My Mother
Played the Piano

My Mother Played the Piano

by
John W. Smith

illustrated by

Tex Stephenson

Published by 20th Century Christian
Nashville, Tennessee

Printed in USA

ISBN #0-89098-138-8

My Mother Played the Piano
© 1993 John W. Smith
Published by 20th Century Christian
Foundation, Nashville, Tennessee

Printed in the United States of America

CONTENTS

Dedication

To all of my early church heroes – the L.C. Utleys, Albert Eslingers and Pink Moodys – men whose faith and faces sustained me in times of temptation and who now have gone to their reward.

To my boyhood friends – Sharon Vincent, Doug Bussey, Tommy and Freddy Petersen and especially to James Macfarland who always tried to do right.

To my students.

To my sisiter Jary, what would I say, what words could tell our journey. God bless you Jary, for all you did, for what you bore, for the understanding and the patience.

To my dear niece, Priscilla, who meant so much to all of us and has gone to be with Jesus.

To my children, Lincoln, Brendan, Kristen and Debbie; Thank you for loving me in spite of everything, and thank you for the joy we have gained through the struggles. This book will let you know who your father was, and I pray it will let you know who you are.

To my parents, W. Fred and Florence M. Smith, who loved me enough to teach me about God, about the church and right and wrong; whose faith formed the foundation of our home and the way we judged value.

To my wife – Judi, who has born with my moods – the terrible crushing depressions and skyrocketing exhilarations – who has moved twenty times without complaining or understanding – who has made a home out of almost nothing and with very little help – who has endured more humiliation, deprivation, rejection, and loneliness than any man has a right to expect.

And above all

I dedicate this book to the glory of the creator of the universe, to His only begotten Son, and to that great Spirit, who yet moves upon the face of the waters – may this book bring praise, glory, honor and adulation from all who read it.

My Mother Played the Piano
The Most Beautiful Song I Ever Heard

MY MOTHER PLAYED THE piano. She played mostly *by ear* I think, but she often looked at the notes too. She played *Red River Valley, When My Blue Moon Turns To Gold Again,* and *Mexicali Rose* - I remember those, but mostly she played church songs. My dad was a member of a church song book, book club of some sort and they were always sending us a new song book. My dad would sit in his chair for hours singing *Do-So-Mi-Do* as he tried to learn all the songs in the new book.

My mom played them on the piano.

It seems now that she mostly played in the early or mid-afternoon. During those summer months, I would approach our little white house and through the open windows, with the white curtains moving with the breeze, I would hear her playing and singing. It was a very comforting - reassuring sound. I'm sure it brought much happiness to her.

Sometimes when I came in to get a drink or some needed thing, or to ask if I could go further than normal, she would say, *John, come here and sing this with me.* She didn't say it like a command or an order or anything - not like when she said, *Go clean the chicken coop,* or *Go hoe the garden.* Those were orders. She would just say it like a request or like she would appreciate it as a favor - you know. I usually didn't want to. I was afraid my friends would hear through the open windows - or worse yet they would say, *What took you so long?* And I would sort of cringe and say, *I was singing some church songs with my mother,* and they would look at me as though my driveway didn't go all the way to the street. I made every possible excuse I could. Of course I didn't just say *no.* You can't do that with requests you know, and besides I didn't say that word to my parents - the *N* word was the death word and if I said it - even in fun, I would die-
I always knew that.

Come on John, she would coax, *it will only take a minute.*

Oh Mom, I would say, *Oh, mother* - the exasperation and disgust would absolutely drip from my voice but usually I would go, dragging my reluctant feet.

She would be so enthusiastic. She would say, *Now, I want you to sing this alto part for me,* and she would play it and sing it and then she would play it while I sang it. Then she would play the soprano part and sing that – then she would play both of them and sing my part and then she would play both parts and I would sing alto while she sang soprano. You can't imagine how excited she would be when we finished. *Isn't that just the prettiest song you ever heard?*, she would exclaim. If I thought it was something less than that,

I certainly kept it to myself.

I played my role halfheartedly at best. I had learned that often the quickest way back outside was to learn my part as rapidly as possible but sometimes I just couldn't get into it and sang so poorly and was so sour faced and sullen that she would slowly close the book, pat me on the shoulder and say, *you go on back to your friends now, we'll do this some other time.* She didn't say it with anger or even resentment and I don't know how many times it happened before I noticed that when I went back outside I didn't hear the piano or singing any more that day.

It wouldn't have cost me much – and it meant so much to her. I look back with regret and tears for my selfishness and insensitivity.

My mother played the piano and sang church songs. Sometimes now, when I can find a place where it is still and allow myself to be very quiet, I can still see the old white house with the white curtains moving at the open windows, and through those open windows I hear her voice and see those nimble fingers moving on the keys.

From this valley they say you are going,
we will miss your bright eyes and sweet smile.
for they say you are taking the sunshine
that has brightened our path for awhile.

Come on John, she coaxes, *it will only take a minute.*
You sing alto - it goes like this - and I'll sing soprano -
Isn't that the most beautiful song you ever heard?

And in my mind I say, *I'm coming Mom,* and I rush to her with joy, because I know how happy it will make her.

And it is, you know,

The most beautiful song

I ever heard.

Introducing the Introduction

I WROTE AN INTRODUCTION because every book is supposed to have one, you know. Of course, very few people ever read introductions because they don't read like the rest of the book. So I thought that I ought to introduce my introduction. If you read my introduction - you mustn't be either encouraged or discouraged - because it's not like the rest of the book. It's really a very good introduction though - I've read it myself and I found it quite interesting and reasonably entertaining.

You might as well go ahead and read it - I mean, you already bought the book - and paid good money for it - it would be a great waste of my time and your money if you didn't.

Introductions tell you in about four or five pages what it takes the rest of the book, two hundred pages to tell you - except that they're sort of dry, stuffy and text bookish. This one is a little better. On a scale of one to ten - it rates a six in my estimation. If you think it rates lower than that - please don't tell me, a person can only take so much rejection.

If you read the introduction and really enjoy it - we're in deep trouble. If you can still get a refund on the book, you probably ought to. If you don't enjoy it - take heart, there is hope for you. I mean - if you say to yourself - *Well, I guess that was okay, but two hundred pages of that would be a little more happiness than I could stand all lumped together in one package,* then proceed in hope.

Introduction

THIS IS A BOOK ABOUT raising children. It didn't start out to be – that just sort of happened. Actually, it's a book about many things, it's about – well, life I guess, but mostly it's a book about God, and parents and children. It isn't a *how to* manual, and it certainly isn't a book written by an eminent psychologist based upon thousands of case studies – God save us from another one of those. As I said, it's a book about life – actually it's about *my* life, which isn't so terribly important except that I'm convinced that there is a thread of commonality in the lives of all of us. When you read this book you're supposed to remember, and those memories should bring a smile to your face, a tear to your eye, a reverence to your heart –

and make you better.

It's a storybook and if you like good stories, I think you'll like this book. Most of these stories are from my childhood – some of them are from my children's childhood, some are from other people's experience. People are always taking me off to the side and asking me if these stories really happened. Now, what kind of question is that? It sure takes the fun out of things. I think what is important is the **truth**. Did the parables that Jesus told really happen? I mean, was there really a pearl merchant who sold all of his pearls to buy one big one? If he did, it sure put him out of business. Stories convey truth. For thousands of years truth was measured by them, and it still is, but not as much. I believe that all of these stories are true in that sense, and in that sense,

they are all parables.

The basic premise of this book is that children are not raised deliberately – that successful parenting is not the direct, mathematical result of premeditated, organized, and intentional planning. Providence, prayer, and the spiritual disposition of the parents have far more influence on the maturation process than most of us would care to acknowledge. I want specifically to encourage parents to pray more, to trust to God's providence more, and to seek to draw themselves more closely into conformity with His will.

One important factor about these stories, that can be easily overlooked because it's so obvious, is the fact that I remember them. Out of the millions of isolated events of my childhood, these stand out clearly. To my parents, the events were probably inconsequential.

They had no suspicion that these incidents would so impact my thinking and form the foundation for my future actions. That is why I say that outside of major patterns, raising children is not done deliberately, because parents do not have the mental and physical power or dedication to deliberately order each day's activities and bring about preplanned results. I do not mean that childrearing is accidental - I do mean that good parenting is much more a result of-

who you are -

than what you do.

If you are trying to prepare yourself for parenting by reading *how to* manuals, you are going to continue to have the same problems that you are having now. It is problems that drove you to the *how to* manuals, that line the shelves of best sellers. *Ah, here it is,* you say, *that's the very thing I need.* And so today and tomorrow you are very conscious of being and doing what the *how to* manual says, but then you get very tired, or sick, or extremely busy and incidents take place when you are least prepared, so you react - as you are bound to react - not like the *how to* manual says, which may or may not be right - but according to your feelings and it blows away all of your best plans, and so you go back to the bookshelves and select another *how to* manual, vowing that you will do better next time.

But you won't, you know.

But, you say, *isn't this just another **how to** manual?* I certainly do not mean it to be so - at least in any specific sense. If it is, it is in the general sense of how to be a better person. What I want to show is not how my parents did things right, or wrong for that matter, but how they constantly grew closer to God; how they operated within His providence; how they set out to be not **better parents** specifically, but to be **better people**. I know that may sound very *iffy,* and vague, but that is a result of the humanistic value system we have incorporated into our parenting. A value system which is *man oriented,* a system which elevates psychology, and scientific human endeavor to a place where we really believe that we can solve all of our problems by simply applying the appropriate formula. While we turn more and more to television, to computers, to the wonders of chemically and psychologically modified and controlled behavior, God keeps saying,

Depend on Me, I'm the only hope you have.

There were great parents - millions of them, before anybody ever thought of writing a *how to* manual or did a psychological study of ninety-seven sets of parents. How do you study parents? By going and living in a home for ten years and observing the daily interaction of the family? The only problem is that you'd be dead before you finished your study. I would defy anyone to really study even one set of parents.

Almost everyone knows by now that no two children are just alike and that they must be treated differently. Not only are no two children alike in a given family - no two are alike in the world. That's why people soon find out that the *how to* manuals don't work.

It is my prayer that quite often, as you read this book, you will find yourself putting it down with a sigh and saying to yourself - because you alone would understand - "Yes, that is exactly the way it was," and it doesn't matter if it was right or wrong, because if it was right, you need to imitate it and if it was wrong, you need to change it. Remembering and reliving and rethinking - that's what this book is about.

A fascinating article from the August 7, 1989 issue of U.S. NEWS AND WORLD REPORT titled, *Dr. Spock Had It Right*, directs itself to several varied psychological approaches that have been vogue in our history. The article concludes with this poignant statement...

> *Although these studies are as objective as anyone can get, they can't bestow upon parents any magic formulas for preventing brattiness or rearing angels. Perhaps the most striking theme to emerge from all the scientific data is that establishing a pattern of love and trust and acceptable limits within each family is what really counts, and not lots of technical details. The true aim of discipline, is not to punish unruly children but to teach and guide them and help instill inner controls. For in the end, as every mother and father know, parenting is far more of an art than a science.*

The only thing that ever works consistently is a nature that has been broadened and tempered by being born again into God's family, and is incorporating His wisdom and nature into its own. Is it really that simple? My goodness no - don't you understand how difficult it is to become like God?

Simple?

I guess not!

Why Is Love So Hard?

THE APOSTLE PAUL says that love is the greatest thing of all, and most folks I believe, would agree. I wonder though - why is it the greatest thing - greater even than hope, or faith? And if indeed it is the greatest thing, why don't things work out better? Why is there so much disappointment, pain and heartache in family relationships,
I mean we all love each other, don't we?

I've never heard a parent say, "I just don't love my children, I've tried, but I just can't make it happen." Is love enough? Would all of our family relationships be positive if love was present? If love is enough, and it is the greatest thing of all, why isn't it easier? I mean, doesn't love just come *naturally* to us? Loving is tough, ask any parent who's really trying and they'll tell you that it takes work - the *natural* part wears off pretty quickly. What they mean is that they love their kids *naturally* - in the big picture - but in the practical, on-going, day to day stuff, they have to work hard at it.

I don't mean love, like in "falling in love," or loving your truck or chocolate pie - that comes easy and *natural* - I mean loving like in, "God so loved the world that He gave His Son," or "husbands love your wives as you love yourself" - that doesn't come *naturally,* you have to work at that. Falling in love is the most primitive and unrealistic form love has - it's the one we talk about most and read about and watch on T.V. and it's the one we want most, because it comes *naturally* and it's so pleasing, delicious and tingly. The problem is that we expect loving to be the same way -
and it's not.

Loving is hard because it isn't always reciprocated - or understood for that matter - and when it's not, you can't just walk away like in falling in love. Loving folks - even children - doesn't mean that they will return it or appreciate it. And you can't make them, no matter how hard you try. That's why children are always saying, "If you loved me, you would, - say **yes** to me," and what they mean is, that in their understanding, when you love somebody you do what they want, and so love becomes a guilt imposing, manipulative tool to be used to gain selfish ends.

Every parent wants to be loved by their children and often they are willing to pay incredible prices in order to get it. They will risk their financial security, or violate their own wisdom and experience, even risk the child's own long term happiness and maturity, for the fleeting satisfaction of gaining their child's fickle affections. How many parents have said, "but we gave her everything," and now there is no response, no gratitude, no love, only more demands.

Love is hard because it makes you say, "no" when everything inside of you wants to say, "yes." Love is hard because it makes you say "yes" when everything inside of you wants to say "no." Love is hard because it risks alienation and it is willing to be misunderstood. Love is hard because it will not risk long term good for short term appreciation. Love is hard because it acts according to its own principles. Love is hard because it makes us behave well when we want to behave badly. Love persists in seeking the good of the beloved - not as the beloved wants, but as love dictates. Nowhere are these truths more critical than in child raising.

This brief and painful illustration will serve well to demonstrate my point. I was a musically talented child, born into a musically talented family. Somewhere, about the age of ten or eleven, my mother decided that I should learn to play the piano. She made great personal sacrifices to provide the instrument and money for lessons.

I hated it - resisted it - fought, argued, pouted and was so thoroughly obstinate that I finally wore her down until she gave in and let me quit. What I would give today if her love had been tougher. What a lifelong loss to me that her love wavered, weakened and finally succumbed to selfishness. She settled for short term peace, purchased at the cost of long term good. Her love was flawed by her failure to respond to her own wisdom and experience because she wanted to save herself and me from the pain of insisting on what was best. She failed to realize that living through the rejection created by an unwanted answer, forms the foundation for leaping to a higher level of loving - one not based on getting what I want. Those who avoid that rejection do so only temporarily and are doomed to experience love only at its lowest, most unrewarding level.

In the gospel of John, chapter fifteen, Jesus instructs His disciples to, "love each other as I have loved you." How does Jesus love us? Let me call your attention to a single chapter in Matthew's gospel – chapter twenty five. It is divided into three sections, the parable of the ten virgins, the story of the talents, and the vision of judgment. In each story there is a happy ending and a sad ending. Jesus welcomes five of the virgins, the five and two talented men, and the sheep, into the joy of salvation – He sends five of the virgins, the one talented man and the goats into eternal condemnation. Does Jesus love all the virgins, all of the talented men and the goats as well as the sheep? It is inadmissible that he does not. Which of His responses is the loving one? Is the heart of Jesus untouched by the pleas of the lost? Jesus loves us enough to say "yes," and to say "no," and we must love each other as He has loved us.

No aspect of parenting appears easier and turns out to be more difficult than that of loving your children. We think that it will come naturally to us, but in reality,

we must work harder at loving
than at anything else.

Kane

HE WAS JUST A FAT LITTLE bundle of loose skin, covered with yellow-gold hair, when we got him. It was the only time I ever paid money for a dog – a lot of money – one hundred twenty-five dollars to be exact. It was precious money, but it was Christmas and the puppy was sort of a family Christmas present. He was a yellow Labrador retriever and we named him Kane.

He was beautiful. Even when he was small and clumsy, tripping over his own – too big for his body – feet, he was beautiful. As he grew and filled the folds of his too large skin, he was a joy to us. When he ran, his powerful muscles rippled under that golden coat and he reminded me of a young lion. He went everywhere with us, he loved the water, he would retrieve anything and he was gentle with the children and with friends.

He wasn't very smart, in fact he was unbelievable stupid. He would have starved to death if we hadn't guided him to his food dish. Teaching him tricks was out of the question, but he was loyal to us, and he was ours,

and we loved him.

My sons and I built him a large pen. We went out to an old abandoned mining shaft and we got a twelve by twelve timber for a corner post and some six by sixes. We stretched some hurricane fencing a neighbor had given us around the posts. It didn't look like much, but it did the job of keeping Kane at home when we were gone.

One day, when Kane was nearly a year old, he ran into the road in front of our house to retrieve something the children had thrown and he was hit by a U.P.S. truck.

They called me at work. I came home immediately and found everyone in tears. They had taken him to the veterinarian. He wasn't dead, but it would have been better if he had been. The vet told me that Kane's shoulder was shattered, two of his legs were broken and he had serious internal injuries. He said he could set the legs, put steel pins in his shoulder, and operate to stop the hemorrhaging. It would cost five hundred dollars and he wouldn't guarantee anything.

I didn't have five hundred dollars. I didn't have fifty. I guess I could have placed some things at risk and borrowed it, but I had a decision to make – one that involved the children's education and our shaky financial future. I decided I couldn't do it. Everything inside of me wanted to save the dog, I wanted to say *yes*, but,

I had to say no.

I told the vet to put Kane to sleep and I went home to explain to my children why Kane had to die. We sat at the kitchen table and the children listened with white, tear-stained faces and large unblinking eyes. It's not easy, you know. How much is a dog's life worth? Children have no way of measuring the value of their dog's life against money. Children only know that they love their dog and that somehow their father's financial failures mean that their dog has to die. It isn't easy to love a father who fails – who doesn't pull the rabbit out of the hat when the chips are down. It is a tribute to my children that they tried to understand – what I didn't understand – they tried to trust me and to love me.

When I had explained to them – they asked no questions – they made no effort to plead or bargain for the life of their pet – they knew their father. They went to their rooms to cry out their grief and I went outside. I thought I was going to explode with frustration and anger at my helplessness. I found a stick that Kane had been retrieving for us and I walked over to the empty pen that had been built with so much care and hope.

I began whacking that 12 X 12 corner post with the stick and I began to cry and to pour out my anguish. My wife came out - her eyes red with tears from consoling the children.

John, she said, *what's wrong?*
It's hell to be poor, I said.
I love my kids as much as any man
and I loved the dog -
more than I wanted to -
I try to live right and do right
but right now I hurt so bad
I could die.

It was a long time ago, but remembering it and writing about it has brought back the ache and the anguish. I did the right thing. I knew it then and I know it now,

but doing the right thing is seldom easy and
loving is very hard.

To My Daughter

As I THOUGHT OF ALL the illustrations I could use - both to establish an identity with you and to create a teaching situation that would bring home forcefully the message about why love is so hard, I remembered the following incident.

I have preached many funerals, waited by the bedside of the terminally ill, counseled hundreds of emotionally disturbed families, held the hands of parents whose children had committed suicide, serious crimes, or were drug addicted - dealt with sexual perversion, alcoholism, loneliness and depression. But among all of those things, nothing ever produced a greater depth of despair than I witnessed and experienced as I prayed with this father, counseled and finally formulated the following letter. The circumstances you can piece together from its content; the details are too lengthy and personal to recount.

I do feel compelled to add this disclaimer. This is a *last resort* letter. It is the culmination of months of intensive struggle and heartache. Every conceivable attempt to compromise, to reach an understanding, to find some common ground, had been exhausted. A time came when a stand had to be made, where compromise would only prolong the agony and postpone the inevitable. The proper time to make this stand was a tough decision. I personally felt that it should have been done earlier in this case, but I am only a man, operating within a wisdom and providence that is so much greater than I am that comparison is ridiculous.

Dear Melissa,

I received your letter three days ago and I thought it best to wait until I had opportunity to consider your request, and to pray. Your decision to proceed with the marriage, as you know, is against my every wish. You have stated once again all of your reasons for your decision. I find nothing that we have not been over before and I repeat that your very reasons display your immaturity and the completely false notions you have about the step you are taking. I sympathize deeply with your feelings of frustration, loneliness and emptiness, but that does not change the fact that you are making a tragic mistake by trying to solve your problems - and Kent's, too, - by marriage.

Melissa, you have asked me to participate in the wedding and to "give you away." I simply cannot, in good conscience, do that. In fact, I have pledged myself not to encourage this marriage in any way. I will not be at your wedding. I realize that I cannot rectify my failure to take a stand on previous occasions by taking one now, but I also realize that giving in one more time cannot be justified by my former cowardice and vacillation.

I'm sure this will make you angry with me. It is useless to plead, as you have pled with me on a thousand other occasions, successfully. It is my prayer that some day you will understand that I have acted more in harmony with my love for you in this case than I have in any other. If there is any real feeling between us, if you have any honor in your heart for me as your father, you will know what this is costing me. Perhaps that will help you to understand how serious an error I believe you are committing, and how earnestly I am seeking to help you to avoid a tragedy so cataclysmic that you will be scarred for life by the consequences.

You know - no, I guess you don't! Your mother and I made the same mistake. We carried the burden of it for twenty years and it finally became more than we could bear. Your unhappy, insecure teenage years were the result of the constant tension between your mom and me. We tried to hold it together for you and your brothers. I'm glad we did - it was far better than the alternatives, but I hope that you can see the misery it caused for all of us. Both of our parents warned us against it, but they lacked the moral fiber to say "no," and to throw the weight of the loss of their presence and support behind it. We might have done it anyway, but at least they would have always known they had obeyed their convictions.

You have made a decision. It is your right to do so, and although I believe it to be a grievous error, I respect your right. I, too, have made a decision based upon greater experience, wisdom and specific knowledge. These decisions are in direct conflict and cannot be resolved. There is no middle ground - no room for compromise. I have listened to all of your reasons, you have listened to mine. If you choose to proceed - you must proceed alone, you simply cannot have it both ways. You have had it your way for so long that I realize how terribly bewildering it must be to you to come up against a wall of this kind. There will be many similar walls for you in the future.

I do not know how this will affect our future relationship. It will always be between us and we will pay a price for that. My attitude toward your marriage will not change the day after the wedding, nor the month or year after. I have no wish to indefinitely close the door on our relationship. I will pray for you every day and I sincerely hope you will pray for me. That will be our common ground for the immediate future. I do not hope that your marriage will fail so that I can be proven correct. You simply have no chance to succeed.

I love you more now than ever before. I have been so totally absorbed with my own problems these last years that I have failed miserably to give you the time and attention you needed. God forgive me for that. I need your forgiveness, too. I stand ready to help - to advise - to do anything that will be to your good, and I will continue to stand ready after this marriage is finalized. If I make an error by being too hard in this one instance, God knows I have made a thousand errors by being too easy previously.

Words fail to express the grief I feel as I write this. I feel the despair that always accompanies failure and our inability to go back. God forgive me. I really do love you - you know, if I didn't, sending this letter would not be tearing me apart.

Dad

Stories like this always ignite our curiosity and we wonder - *What happened?* There are two points I want to make as I keep you in suspense about that. First, no matter what happens - it will not *justify* the sins that created the situation. Second, movie makers have the luxury of making their stories turn out as they wish - real life is seldom that way. We all want *happy endings* – unfortunately we do not wish to pay the price that is required.

No conclusion has been reached. The jury is still out. Although the marriage has been postponed, the situation is no different. It is my conjecture that there are wounds here, that under the very best of circumstances will take years to heal and may not even then, completely.

If you would have asked this father, at any point during his daughter's formative years, if he loved her, his immediate and decisive answer would have been "Yes," and he would have believed that with all of his heart. Every parent needs to see the implications of that. **Thinking** that you love someone and even **saying** it, do not mean that you do. Love needs *definition*, and if our definitions are not according to divine truth, then even what we call love, will lead us astray.

If you had asked this father how he knew that he loved her, I'm sure his response would have been centered around the feeling of affection he had for her and the way he provided for her. What I want you to see is that neither of those led him to share practically and emotionally in his daughter's life. They were strangers, living in the same house – love does not behave in that way. His love failed them, because it did not build a trusting, respectful and intimate relationship. Rather, their relationship was one of mutual manipulation, and they both paid a terrible price for it.

Son, Don't Go

PERHAPS NO MORE meaningful definition of love is given to us than in John's gospel.

*For God **so loved** the world*
*That **He gave** his **only** begotten*
Son...

How much **pain** is in that **giving**, which was generated by His **loving**. The rest of the John 3: passage says;

That whosoever believes in Him
should not perish.

That – *whosoever believes* – means that God gave folks a choice and when you've sacrificed as much as He did to give people a choice and they choose wrongly it really hurts.

Love is hard because it makes you hurt. God speaks through the prophet Hosea concerning His beloved people Israel.

> *I cared for you in the desert,*
> *In the land of burning heat.*
> *When I fed them, they were*
> *satisfied;*
> *when they were satisfied, they*
> *became proud;*
> *then they forgot me.*

What a graphic tale of loneliness and despair is told in those words. It is a tale experienced by every parent, a tale of ingratitude, of love not reciprocated.

Love is hard because it makes you say *yes*, when everything inside of you wants to say *no*. Chapter fifteen of Luke's gospel contains the treasured story of the prodigal son and the loving father. The son comes to the father and asks for his inheritance. The father knows why he wants it. The father **can** say *no* – he **wants** to say *no* – everything inside of him tells him to say *no* and saying *no* would be the *easiest* thing to do. The father **knows** the perils of the world – he knows where the boy is going and he knows what can happen there. He knows that sin is fun and that devotion to sensuality is both destructive and addictive. He knows that the boy may not ever come back – either because he has no desire or because he can't – death is a real possibility. The father knows all of the possible outcomes – but he also knows that there is no other way – he says, *OK,*

> *if that's what you really want.*

The father gives him the money and the boy packs his belongings and leaves. The father follows him down the driveway to the road and watches the boy's back as the distance between them grows. He wants to cry out – *Son, don't go! Son, don't go! Stay here with me – we'll work something out.*

But he bears his grief in silence.

The son is totally unaware of his father. His excitement over getting out on his own – having his own apartment – selecting his own friends – getting up and going to bed whenever he wants – having no one to boss him around – the allurement of unrestrained sensual pleasure – the power of youth and plenty of money – all of these keep his attention focused on the road before him. He doesn't even turn around and wave – he doesn't know the pain that is in his father's heart – he doesn't know what love is – but he's going to learn.

Love is hard because the answers aren't always the same. Loving means that you have to give the answer that is best for the one you love and that you never sacrifice long term good, for short term happiness – that you never buy your own peace at the expense of the beloved's failure to achieve their maximum potential. Love risks personal loss, loneliness – even rejection.

Most of us don't love very well – we keep wanting it to be easy – we demand that it be easy – and when it's not, we walk away and call it something else. We need badly to remember that those who don't love enough to experience the heartache of rejection and doubt as they stand in the road and watch their children go – prove themselves unworthy of the overwhelming joy that comes from standing in the same road and –

seeing them come home.

Parental Consent
"Oh, You Men"

WE LIVED AT 3524 ROCHESTER Road in Royal Oak, Michigan. I was a freshman in high school, trying out for the football team. My coach had given me a parental permission form that my mother and father had to sign in order for me to play, and a form to be filled out by a doctor which said that I was healthy enough to be kicked, knocked down, beaten and pounded mercilessly with no permanent damage to my body.

I didn't want to take either form home. We were given a week to have them filled out and returned. I kept them both in my locker. After the week was up, every day before practice the coach would say, *The following people have not turned in their forms,* and he would read this list. At first there were a lot of names on it and it didn't bother me too much, but every day the list grew shorter and my name became more and more conspicuous. Finally, there were only two of us, a Jehovah's witness boy and me.

The coach called us in before practice on Wednesday and told us that if we didn't have the forms turned in by Friday – he simply could not allow us to practice anymore. He was a very nice man, for a football coach, one of the most decent coaches I ever had. He asked us if there was a problem and both of us were embarrassed, because we didn't want to talk about it. The Jehovah's witness boy said that his parent's religious convictions were a major obstacle. The coach wanted us both to play pretty badly – the Witness boy was a very promising player – so he told him he would talk to his parents.

I told him that my mother didn't know that I was practicing for football and that she was strictly opposed to my playing. I also, finally, told him that we had no money for me to get a physical from a doctor. It was eight dollars, I still remember. He said that he would take care of the physical, but it was up to me to get my mother's signature.

Well, the worst possible thing happened in practice that afternoon. We were running a simple tackling drill which was designed to teach us how to knock the ball loose from the runner by using our helmets. Somehow, I caught my cheekbone right on the shoulder pad of the runner I was tackling. The collision removed a patch of skin about the size of a silver dollar. It really wasn't serious at all, but the red, raw, exposed flesh looked terrible.

Of course when I got home it all came out. My mother was working and she didn't get home until 5:30 or 6:00, so it had been pretty easy to disguise my whereabouts after school. When I came in the door, she was home. I had the forms in my hand and my speech ready, but I didn't get to give it.

What happened to your face?, she said, and there was some urgency in her voice.

I was playing football with some guys after school, I hedged, which was sort of true.

How many times have I told you not to play that game? It's just too rough. You've told me several times.

I didn't mention the forms. I went to my room and waited for my dad to get home.

After supper my dad always read the newspaper in the living room while my mother cleaned the kitchen. I took the parental consent form to him and explained that I needed his signature. Although my facial laceration had been quite a topic at supper, he took the form, told me to get a pen and he signed it.

I have to have mom's signature too, I explained.

Sure, he said, *take it to her and tell her I said to sign it.* He returned to his newspaper.

I took it into the kitchen, explained briefly, and showed her where to sign. She got real upset, said she wasn't going to do any such thing and that I must be crazy asking her. I showed her where dad had signed it and told her that he said that she should.

Well, she said, *you can tell him that he must be crazy too.*

I went back into the living room

She won't sign it, I said, he put the paper down.

Did you tell her I said to?

Yes, I said.

What did she say?

She said that you must be crazy.

Let me have that form.

Yes, sir, I said.

He took the card and went into the kitchen, I followed, heart in my mouth. I didn't know what to expect, but what happened was certainly not expected. My mother was standing at the sink with her back to us moving the dishes around in the soapy water – she wasn't washing them, she was just moving them around. Her shoulders were shaking, her eyes were closed, and she was crying. Big tears ran down her face and plopped in the dishwater. She wasn't sobbing or making noise, she was just crying, real quietly. I knew by the way she was crying – by the way her shoulders were slumped – that she was going to sign the form. She wasn't angry or defiant, she didn't have her teeth set and her shoulders squared for a fight. She had already given up. My dad walked over and put his hands on her shoulders and he said, *Florence, it's for the best, he's got to have a chance to prove himself.*

Oh, you men, she said, and there was a lot of disgust in what she said that I didn't understand then, and only understand a little of now – but you wives and mothers out there – you know what, *Oh, you men,* means.

She dried her eyes and her hands on her apron and she took the form from my dad and sat down at the kitchen table. It was only a card table – one of those cardboard kind with the folding legs – in the tee-tiniest kitchen you can imagine. She sat down, and she read the form – every word. There were several clauses in there about in case of injury who to contact, was I allergic to any medication, the name of our family doctor; if hospitalization was required where should I be sent – stuff like that which makes a person apprehensive. She picked up the pen, and then she started to cry again and I

27

thought she had changed her mind, but she signed it and the tears splashed right on the form. She looked up at me and she said, *Go on! Go on, play football and knock your teeth loose and break your nose - for what? Well, I don't have to watch, and I won't.* Then she put her face in her hands and she really cried, but she didn't and she wouldn't.

It was a long time ago. I can still see the tee-tiny kitchen and my mother with her face in her hands, and the tears splashing on the parental consent form. I can still see her drying her eyes on her apron - you know moms don't much wear aprons anymore - they just put real pretty ones on the kitchen wall to make it look "country," but they never put them on. I guess it's because of microwaves and automatic dishwashers - it's a great loss because moms are often best remembered in their aprons. I can still hear her say,

Oh, you men!

I was learning about marriage and about mothers and fathers and God, too. I didn't know it, I didn't mean to learn, and my parents didn't stage the scene in order to teach me a valuable lesson or to create a memory, but I watched them love each other that evening, and me too, because that's how it works. Only I didn't know that was love until much later when I took my oldest son's parental consent form to his mother for her signature. Some things don't change - the doctor's fee had and there was an additional insurance form. But his mother cried and said,

Oh, you men.

Fathers

I FIRMLY BELIEVE THAT THE earliest and often the most critical and lasting notions about what God - our Heavenly Father - is like, in a practical sense, are formed by those same notions about our earthly father. The general impression of who our earthly father is - the overall notions which his presence suggests - dictate the way in which we respond to his directives and honor his wisdom, and so it is with our Heavenly Father. Those notions begin very early and take shape slowly, expanding and being redefined with specific incidents, maturity and perspective. I think of my father much differently now, than I did when he died in 1963.

The challenge to today's fathers is to be worthy of the name. Our culture has eroded and demeaned both traditional and biblical concepts, leaving only frustration and confusion. Fathers, who are half apologetic for bringing their children into the world; so concerned with their children's self-image that they teach them nothing; so afraid of being thought a tyrant or even worse, out of touch, that they fail to discipline them; who want to be a buddy more that they want to be a father, who bow to their every whim rather than risk offending them or even more likely - leave parenting to their wives - are very misleading examples of divine fatherhood.

What is a father? Fathers have jobs - they bring home money. Father's work - when they're sick, when they hate their jobs, and when they see no hope.

Fathers are fixers. They can fix anything - plumbing, bicycles, lawnmowers and toy trucks. And when they can't fix it - they say that they don't have the right tools, or that we needed a new one anyway, or they don't make them like they used to. They even fix cuts, bruises and disappointments -

or make them unimportant.

Fathers are not afraid of the dark, the neighbor's dog or the boogie man.

Fathers long to be the boys they once were - and never will be again -

but they never stop trying.

Fathers are story tellers. Almost everything that happens reminds them of another time and in those stories, they stop being business men, plumbers, factory workers and professionals. In those stories - they are real and their children see a vision of what "was" that makes what "is" much different.

Fathers are decision makers - they always know where they're going. Fathers are leaders, they accept responsibility even when they go wrong and they defy a culture that seeks to emasculate and feminize them and turn them into junior partners on the family board of directors.

Fathers provide spiritual leadership for their families. They are not ashamed to be seen praying or reading their Bibles. They are careful to act and talk in harmony with scriptural injunctions and precedents - and when they go wrong - they admit their error, ask forgiveness, pray about it, and leave it behind them.

The Bible portrays four major characteristics of God that every father should emulate. First, God is dependable and consistent. God keeps His word - either "yes," or "no" or "not now." Second, He is understanding. When we say, "it wasn't my fault," He can say, "yes it was" or, "I know it wasn't" or, "it really doesn't matter does it!" Third, He is forgiving, which means that sometimes I don't get what I deserve and sometimes I do, but in either case, when He forgives, its over. Fourth, God is loving and that means that He always acts in my best interests.

What kind of father are you?

What notions about God do your children have?

And to My Children
I Bequeath

MY FATHER, WILLIAM FRED SMITH, was born on June 19, 1897. He was born in the city of Poughkeepsie, township of Strawberry, County of Sharp, state of Arkansas. His mother, Suzanne Clementine Smith, was 29 when he was born and he was her seventh child.

He was born at home.

He told me that he finished the tenth grade in school, which he said, was all the grades there were, and he never had any further education. He had great admiration for his teacher - Cecil Picken, whom he mentioned often.

He was inducted into the U.S. Army on October 31, 1918, but the war was soon over, so he was discharged on December 24, 1918. He was in the 43rd Company, 11th Battalion, 162nd Depot Brigade. He was one of the nameless, faceless, lack luster privates who never went anywhere or did anything and who consequently never had any stories to tell.

He married my mother on October 4th, 1930 in Detroit, Michigan. He was thirty three. On their marriage license he listed his employment as, *Gas Station Operator.*

My sister, Lillian Clementine, was born April 26, 1931 and I was born on March 31, 1937.

William Fred Smith died in Veteran's Hospital in Indianapolis, Indiana at 3:30 p.m. on October 10, 1963.

My father was the most ordinary, unexceptional, unsuccessful man you can imagine. He was always in debt - he consistently made bad business decisions - he kept our family in constant turmoil with ill-conceived moves - he quit good jobs and took bad ones. My mom and dad had marital problems - sometimes serious ones. When you live in constant turmoil, moving from town to town with financial ruin facing you and the future holding no hope but a cycle of repetition, there is bound to be trouble. My mom *left home* two or three times - I think from sheer desperation, trying to find relief from the hopeless cycle of poverty and drudgery which surrounded her. I still don't know where she went. My dad would say - *Mom is gone for a few days.* Then she would call and my dad would go and get her and bring her back.

My dad never left home.

My dad loved to fish - he never had the time - or the money - or equipment and he didn't really know much about it. When we went, it was to Bogie Lake – out near Commerce. We rented a boat from old man Bogie and we rowed all over the lake. Sometimes we caught some blue gills and sunfish and bullheads. We kept everything we caught and we ate them. The few times we went I remember – I remember nearly everything about it. About the time we got to where we might have gone more – he died.

Mothers are most appreciated when you're small and when you're growing up. Fathers don't get appreciated until much later. Sometimes you have to be fifty or sixty before you really understand. Fathering never stops – and some of the most important fathering my dad ever did was when I was grown.

What I'm trying to say – what I want you to see – is that my father failed in just about everything – in the army, in education, in sports, at work, in financial matters – in just about everything. The homes we lived in were often humiliating. We even had to depend upon the charity of others.

There were only two or three things that were constant in my life. We always prayed before meals – no matter where we lived or how little we had. We always went to church. Church was the glue that held our family together. It wasn't just services, it was singings, potlucks, work days, Bible studies, gospel meetings, weddings and funerals. And my dad never grumbled about going – he was always happy – expectant.

The third thing that was constant was that my dad worked every day. It was absolutely heroic. Under the most hopeless circumstances he never quit. He got up and went to work every day. He had two marvelous gifts – a great singing voice and he had a great gift for hope. He always believed that something good was going to happen to him. He went to the mailbox every day – expecting it. He didn't know exactly what it was but he always believed it would come. It never did – but that isn't important because,

his hope kept him going.

I said it never came – well, actually that isn't true. On October 10, 1963, at Veteran's Hospital in Indianapolis, Indiana, at about 3:30 p.m. he went to the mailbox for the last time – and when he opened it – it was there. The thing he had been looking for and hoping for and expecting all of his life. I wish I could have seen his face when he opened it.

Yes, dad failed in everything with one exception. He succeeded in the only thing that matters. I am what I am today, not because of his failures, but because of his only success. If he had succeeded in **every other** area, and failed in this one, he would have truly been a failure.

When my dad died, he left us nothing – unless of course you think that singing and going to church and praying before meals and living in hope, are really worth something.

What do you plan to leave your children?

Jump

ONE DAY I HAD BEEN PLAYING in our backyard with a paint can lid. It was before the days of frisbees, and perhaps the inventor of the frisbee got his idea from watching the creative genius of a child who, like me, had discovered the amazing flying propensities of a paint can lid. I was sailing it into the wind and as its momentum slowed, the wind would take it higher and higher and then it would begin its downward and backward glide and I would try to catch it. Eventually it landed and lodged on the roof of the chicken coop. I fretted and worried most of the afternoon trying to dislodge it. We had no ladder and I finally gave up.

When my father came home, I met him in the driveway. Before he was out of the car, I began pleading with him to help me to retrieve my toy. He put his lunch pail down on the front porch and we walked around the house together. He assured me that it was no problem and that we could get it back.

He hoisted me up on his shoulders – then grabbed my feet and boosted me up onto the roof of the chicken coop. He told me to walk very carefully because the coop was old and decaying. I retrieved my toy and returned to the edge of the coop. I felt very powerful looking down at my father. He smiled up at me and then held out his arms and said,

jump.

I close my eyes and I can see him now, forty five years later, as plainly as I can see the lake and the trees from where I sit writing this just now. He was so tall, so strong, so confident with his big, handsome, grinning face, that it is easier for me to imagine that day than the day he died. I jumped, with no hesitation I jumped and he caught me easily and hugged me and then swung me to the ground.

He sent me to retrieve his lunch pail and in a moment we were in the house and the incident was forgotten – no, it wasn't forgotten was it? He would be amazed that I remember it – I'm sure that within a very short time he forgot it. He wasn't trying consciously to be a good father. He didn't come home that day with a plan to create a lasting memory for his son. It wasn't planned at all.

My point to you parents is that most parenting cannot be planned for, except in your own personal walk with God and in prayer. Many great opportunities for lasting impressions are either lost or become negatives because you can't fake what you are when the unexpected comes.

If my father had generally been selfishly unconcerned with his children's cares, there would have been no time nor cause for him to turn this unexpected moment into a great triumph – he would have acted according to his nature, told me he was much too tired to fool with me, reprimanded me for my carelessness and gone into the house leaving me to my own devices, and the moment would have been lost.

The opportunities come – unexpectedly, unplanned for, and most of the time we react according to our nature. We serve our children best by seeking to constantly become more closely molded into the image of our Lord Jesus Christ – not by reading *how to* manuals on child rearing. We do not become good parents by trying to practice a parenting philosophy which is contrary to our natures. We become good parents – good neighbors, good husbands and good friends by becoming *good*, by turning our lives toward God.

Love's Old Sweet Song

Just a song at twilight   When the heart is weary
When the lights are low   Sad the day and long
And the flickering shadows, Still to us at twilight
come and softly go   comes love's old sweet song.

DURING THE YEAR THAT WE LIVED on Gardenia Street in Royal Oak, I got very sick. I think it was some sort of influenza but the Smith's didn't *doctor* much, so we never knew. We accepted our sicknesses as a part of God's divine providence and we worked our way through them as best we could. We cured everything with chicken noodle soup, dry toast, poached eggs and hot tea. (I highly recommend this remedy to all physicians who read this) of course there were cold washcloths for fever.

I had been sick for several days and my vomiting, fever and inability to eat or drink had made me very weak. My mother had stayed at my bedside, or close by, the entire time. My dad was working at some kind of tool and die shop, so I only saw him in the evenings. He would stick his head in the door to see if I was awake – if I was, he'd grin real big and say, *Hey, bud, how you doing?* He said it so cheerfully that it made me feel better. That was at first. Toward the end, when I was so sick and weak that I could scarcely speak, and they had begun to worry, he'd come in and take my hand, or rumple my hair a little and he'd say, *How you feeling, son?* His face would be filled with care, and I was sorry to worry him so.

One night, very late, I awoke slowly from my feverish sleep. The light was on in the hallway and the door to my room was open just a crack. In the shadowy half-light I could see someone sitting by my bed. I thought it was my mother. I must have moved a little because I felt someone squeeze my hand. I knew it wasn't my mother. The hand was large, strong and rough. Without turning my head, I moved my eyes slowly in his direction. He was sitting – slumped over in a chair. He still had his work clothes on – a light blue shirt and dark blue pants with heavy black shoes and white socks. There were stains on the shirt and it smelled that kind of burned oil smell that saturated all of his shop uniforms. His head was resting in his hand, his eyes were closed and there were tears on his face. When I saw his lips move a little, I knew immediately that he was praying.

My dad was singing, *Love's Old Sweet Song,* not those words, and not music, you understand – but the oldest, sweetest song there is. A song that has been sung since the beginning of time. When my heart is weary, sad the day, and long – at twilight I remember those days and love's old sweet song. My dad was singing it at its very best. I was eleven.

It is important to see that those events paid – more than paid for all of his failures. Fathers can fail much – and often – and they do – even the best of them. But when the big moments come – the real crises – they have to be there. And this is really important. You never know when they will come, you *can't just show up for the big moments*

– you have to show up every day and be there for all of the little moments – the ones that don't get remembered – that's the price you pay to get to be there when that providential opportunity presents itself –

to create a memory.

Sometimes you have to fail a thousand times to succeed just once. And if you do, that big success becomes the climax to the failures – and the failures aren't really failures anymore – they're just the parental training ground and even a child understands that you have to practice, and that if you don't, you strike out with the bases loaded.

Nowadays we talk about *quality* time. I hear people say inane things like, *Well, I don't get to spend a lot of time with my kids, but what I do spend I make sure is quality time.* What hogwash! We can rationalize anything. How do we *make sure* that it's *quality* time? What is quality time to a child? Is help with history quality time? Is sitting up with a sick child quality time? Is saying grace before meals quality time? And don't you have to **be** there? You simply do not have the power to *create* quality time. Those moments are providential. *Being there* consistently is the only guarantee of being there when those moments come.

Remember that one of God's most impressive qualities is that;
He is the God
who is **there**.

The Upward Way

THE BOY WAS SHORT AND HE still had much of what is called, *baby fat* in his appearance. He wore glasses and was often teased. His school record was far from brilliant, except that he was favored by his teachers because he was well mannered and said, *Sir* and *Ma'am*. His father and mother were concerned because he had no victories. He never won at anything. He couldn't make any of the teams, he lacked aggressiveness and he seemed to be constantly withdrawing. He had little enthusiasm for life and he was alone much.

Behind the house where they lived, were some high mountains

topped by great jagged upthrusts of perpendicular rock, which overlooked the countryside. The steep slopes beneath were extremely rugged and forbidding, covered with pin oak brush, cat claw, cactus, manzanita, ironwood and ponderosa pine with an occasional blue spruce. The washes, which carried the spring run off, cut deep ravines in these slopes and were choked with huge boulders, fallen ages ago, log jams of fallen trees, brush and other debris, and in many places nearly vertical, smooth, water worn rock inclines which were impassable. The father noticed that the boy looked often toward those craggy summits, gazing long minutes in wonder at their majesty. One winter day, when the sun was glistening radiantly from the peaks that were covered with snow, the boy expressed his desire to some day climb to the top. The father determined that his chance would come.

Accordingly, one fine spring day – with no warning – the father announced that there would be no school that day – a special project was planned. The excitement, the anticipation, as they filled canteens, packed a lunch, dressed appropriately in *climbing clothes*, was well worth the effort. They drove up the mountain as far as the last rut-riddled road would take them – found a promising ravine and set out. It was daylight when they began.

Those who mounted Everest worked no harder, suffered no greater hardship, discouragement – had no greater desire to quit. The father had not realized how difficult a task he had set, but he knew they must not fail, the boy must accomplish this. The boy, red-faced from exertion, panting hoarsely, sweating profusely – hinted more than once that perhaps they ought to return.

The heroic ascent continued.

Twice they broke out into the open, and the panorama of the miles that they could see was awesome. Their whole town, tucked away in a fold of lesser hills, looked insignificant. *I'll bet we can see Flagstaff from the top*, the boy cried, and they plunged ahead.

At the second opening they stopped and ate part of the lunch. They rested their weary backs and aching legs against a great ponderosa. They shared a tree, a sandwich, a canteen, a view, a struggle, a hope, their fatigue, and they shared the marvelous silence. *It sure is quiet, isn't it, Dad? I never heard it so quiet before.*

They were close, and it was good.

There was no talk of returning now. When they finally, reluctantly, but with renewed vigor, left their lunch spot, they only talked of how long – how far to the top. They reached it by eleven o'clock.

39

The last seventy-five yards was hand by hand climbing up a vertical, rock ribbed surface. When they reached the top, their hearts were pounding and they were absolutely breathless. The father had come behind, to help the boy, to reassure him against falling, and because he wanted him to be first. When the boy finally topped the ascent he paused and turned, stretching out his hands, his long brown hair moving with the wind, - some of it stuck to the sweat of his forehead - and he said,

Let me help you up, Dad, it's great.

Even here, although a basic plan was made, there could be no preparation for what might possibly happen along the way since the father had not made the trip before. We can purpose to do good, but the actual doing is always a reaction to the providential opportunities which He affords.

This Is My Son

When Israel was a child, I loved him…
I taught Ephraim to walk, taking them
by their arms; but they did not know
that I healed them…
My people are bent on backsliding from Me…
How can I give you up Ephraim?..
My heart churns within Me,
My sympathy is stirred.   Hos. 11:

WE WERE ON OUR WAY to take our oldest son to his first year at college. We had decided to take a brief vacation and visit some dear friends we had not seen in some time. We drove to the school, eight hundred miles away, dropped off his car and all of his possessions and continued on our way. It was a happy, carefree time. We had been singing together since the children were small, and as we drove we rehearsed our entire repertoire of songs over and over.

Our visit passed, much too quickly, and now we found ourselves returning to the college where we would leave our first-born. The closer we got, the quieter it became, the singing stopped and our

words were tense and apprehensive. It really began to dawn on us that our family was breaking up for the very first time and that things would never be the same.

The time came. We dreaded it, hated it, wished to avoid it, but it came. We stood in the college parking lot beside his car, quiet, embarrassed, grieving, at a loss for words. Finally I said, *Son, say goodbye to your sister.* I tried to keep the huskiness from my voice but it was useless. They embraced and her face was wet with tears. *Say goodbye to your brother.* It was done, these two who had fought and argued. They held to each other as though they had always been best of friends. *Say goodbye to your mother.* My voice was a raspy whisper now and I had lost control. They cried and held each other for a long time. And then it was my turn. He put his arms around my neck and he said,

I love you, Dad.

The finest words a man ever heard. The words that pay for the sleepless nights, the overdrawn checking account, the empty gas tank, the unmade bed, the uncut grass, the undumped garbage, the gray hairs, and the, *will he ever grow up?* They pay for the thoughtlessness, the ring in the tub, and the, *I'll be right back. I love you, Dad,* it pays for it all, because what else is there? What else could pay? What else could you hold in your heart? What else could you take to your hospital bed and to your death? *I love you, Dad.* That will last. You can spend some of that every day for the rest of your life and your account will be larger when you die, than when you opened it, because the interest on love is very high and always exceeds any withdrawals.

When it was done, when there was nothing to do but leave, we drove slowly away. I was leaving my son in the hands of strangers, in a strange city. As we drove from the campus, I had an overwhelming urge to stop and get out. I wanted to stand in the middle of the lawn and scream at the buildings,

This Is My Son!

Do you know what that means to me? I'm leaving him here with you, please respect him and take care of him. This is my son. I have earned the right to say it by raising him and caring for him all of these years. What happens to him, happens to me. What you do to him, you do to me.

God has given me this precious insight into His own feelings when Jesus was born in Bethlehem of Judea. The great star, the heavenly choir, the wise men, the angels who appeared – these are all His way of announcing to the world – *This Is My Son, I'm leaving Him here with you. He's the best I've got, please honor and respect Him, and remember, what you do to Him, you do to Me.* This affirmation is repeated at the baptism of Jesus, again at the transfiguration and finally at the cross. Each time, the voice of the Father affirms, *This Is My Son, I'm proud of Him, and I acknowledge Him as My Son, My only begotten, respect Him.*

An integral part of knowing God is understanding His feelings. He feels as we do, for we are made in His image. His feelings are separated from ours in degree and they are not flawed by the flesh, but He grieves as we grieve; He feels loss as we do, and restoration fills His great heart just as it fills ours. In the final analysis what do I want from my children? I want them to love me – nothing else will satisfy. Yes, of course, I want them to respect me and obey me, but unless they love me, their respect and their obedience is empty.

If my son offered me a check for a half-million dollars and said, *There Dad, now we're even,* I know what I would say – *Son, me and you are never going to be even - you haven't got enough to get even with me. If you think you can pay for what your mother and I have invested in you with money - you've got a lot to learn about love.* It was love that created the universe – it was love that created man – it was love that gave us a choice and it was love that said we must die because we chose wrongly. It was love that created endless possibilities by sending Jesus to die for us and there is only one acceptable response to God's love.

> Teacher, which is the greatest commandment?
> 'Love the Lord your God with all your heart
> and with all your soul and with all your mind.
> This is the first and the great commandment.'
> Matt. 22:37

God will never be satisfied with anything less than love and everything else is less than that because love is the greatest thing of all.

I love you, Dad.

Which Kind Are You?

JUDI WENT INTO THE WINN-DIXIE to buy a few items we needed. It was totally dark, and it was raining. I parked where I could see both store exits, so that when she came out, I could pick her up. For this time of night there were a lot of shoppers. I opened my window about three inches to keep it from fogging.

There was a Chevy station wagon parked pretty close to me, and as I waited, the family who owned it came out. They had their sacks of groceries in a shopping cart. There were five of them – husband and wife, about thirty-five, he was pudgy and balding – she was sort of plain vanilla, except her hair. The rain and the gentle glow of the vapor lights in the parking lot, caused it to shine nice and soft and curly all over her head and neck and down into her face. I wanted to tell her how pretty it was, but I didn't. They had a boy, about ten, I guess. He was pushing the cart. He looked about right – jeans, tee shirt and Reeboks. There were two nondescript others – about four and six maybe, but their gender will forever remain a mystery.

The father opened the tailgate of the station wagon and he and the boy unloaded the cart. When they finished, the father said, *Run the cart over there to the collecting area, Danny.*

It was raining – not hard though – it wasn't offensive, just a sort of warm, pleasant drizzle that makes you want a good book, someone you love, and the leisure to be drowsy.

The boy didn't want to. It was about forty yards. I could hear them plainly and I'm sure they never noticed me.

Aw, Dad, it's raining, he complained.

It will only take a second and it won't hurt you. But there was no conviction in his voice, the father was reasoning with the boy – treating him as an equal.

The boy took full advantage.

Those people over there didn't put theirs back, he argued, pointing to several carts carelessly left in various places.

We're not responsible for them, just for us, the father rejoined.

But who cares? the boy replied, *they got people hired to come out here and collect these carts.*

The mother, tired of waiting, now joined in on the boy's side.

For heaven's sake, Carl, come on! One more cart in the parking lot won't change the history of the world.

The boy sensed victory and opened the door to get in. The father shrugged his shoulders in defeat and put his hand on the door handle. Then he stopped. At first I couldn't figure out why, but I followed his eyes across the misty parking lot and I saw what he saw - an elderly couple, her arm in his, pushing their cart slowly, toward the collecting area. It caused a whole transformation in him. When he spoke there was firmness and authority in his voice - even his posture straightened, his chin lifted and his shoulders squared a little. I suspect he looked much like the man he had been when he got married.

Danny, he said, *come here.* He came.

Do you see those carts that are "in" the cart collecting area? There are two kinds of people, Danny, those who put their carts away, and those who don't. In this family, Danny, we put our carts away because that's the kind of people we are. Don't ever forget that, Danny. Now put that cart where it belongs.

As the boy directed the cart to its appropriate place, it occurred to me how right the father was. There are two kinds of people, in every area of life - two kinds of people - two kinds of fathers.

Which kind are you?

Will He Give Him A Stone?

Or what man is there among you who,
if his son asks for bread, will he
give him a stone? Matthew 7:7-12

IT'S FUNNY HOW THINGS work out. Special things, things you would never think to ask for, things you couldn't possibly plan for - and if you're not careful you don't even realize what a special gift has been sent your way and so you miss much of the blessing.

I took my last two children to Lubbock, Texas for college. It's a thousand miles from Montgomery to Lubbock. One is a senior, but has never been away from home. The other is a freshman - our baby - the last. The last one is like the first one - but different too. It's a thousand miles to Lubbock. My excuse for going was that I needed to haul their stuff - which was enough to fill at least one freight car

– but it was more than that – I wanted to hang on to them – even for just two or three more days. I was buying time. The inevitable good-bye was a constant oppression.

We arrived Monday afternoon and they got settled. On Tuesday evening, I told them I would pick them up at 8:30 Wednesday morning to help them start registration, then I was going to head home. I couldn't sleep Tuesday night, so I got up and wrote each of them a note. I went in the darkness to the place they were staying – pinned the notes to the door – and left. I haven't run from many things in my life – there were many times when I should have and didn't – but I ran from this one – I just couldn't do it.

Slowly – tearfully, alone, I drove away.

It's forty miles to Post from Lubbock, and before I got there the sun began to rise. It doesn't rain often in West Texas – if you listen to the farmers, it rains like most folks go to church – Christmas and Easter – but it was raining when I left. For those of you not familiar with West Texas, I must explain something. Those of you who do know West Texas can skip this part. West Texas is **Flat**. The most conspicuous – the most striking feature – the most absolutely mind boggling, eye blinking aspect of the landscape, is its amazing **flatness**. You can see much of the world from West Texas. People who live there think you can see **all** of it. The names of the towns will help you to understand the area. Read these names slowly; Brown-field, Shallow-water, Post, Littlefield, Earth, Plain-view, Level-land, White-face, Ropes-ville, Pan-handle. These are graphic names. The people who originated them were honest, God-fearing folks who wouldn't tell a lie. Their children haven't done so well. Back to my story!

Driving to Post, off to my left (to the East), without a single obstruction except for a few oil derricks, is a glorious sunrise, as clear, as totally unclouded as anything you can imagine. Off to my right (to the West), over fields of cotton stretching as far as your imagination will carry you, is a driving rainstorm. In between, ascending in a high arc from North to South, from horizon to horizon, is a rainbow. I want to use some adjectives, I want to say brilliant, spectacular, magnificent, none of them will do. In fact, it was a double rainbow. One was absolutely clear, with distinct and unmistakable colors; the other, its shadow, was misty and vague. I could see both ends – from ground to ground. I stopped, got out, and just looked. I tried to take pictures, but I couldn't get all of it, not even with a wide angle lens.

If I could tell you how hope rose in me – how I felt that God, my Father, was laying His hand on my shoulder and saying –

I know how you feel, I had to say good-bye to My Son one time, it nearly broke My heart. I was thinking of you this morning and this is just a little "going away" present from Me to you. I thought you'd like it. Lots of other folks will enjoy it, but really it was just for you. I'm going to take it away now, but

> *I hope it meant something to you,*
> *and that you will remember it.*

It was gone. One minute it was there – the next it was gone – without a trace. It will live in my heart and mind forever.

What an insight into the nature of divine fatherhood, and what an example for earthly fathers.

My children awoke fully expecting me to be there, instead they found a note. I believe that my absence conveyed more than my presence could have. I believe that my simple note of love and understanding communicated in a far more lasting way my feelings for them. God responded to my prayers with a totally unexpected token of love and assurance, because he saw a much bigger picture than I did. I had prayed for **strength**, for **faith**, and **assurance**. I wonder how many times I have asked for healing and missed the medicine. I wonder how many times I have pouted, and doubted because I thought He didn't care, when the problem was with my eyes, and ears, and heart.

It is every father's obligation to constantly see a bigger picture than his children see and to react according to his vision, not theirs. In so doing, he gently opens their eyes to what he sees.

> *If you then, being evil, know how to*
> *give good gifts to your children, how*
> *much more will your Father who is in*
> *heaven give good things to those who*
> *ask Him.*

Just the Two of Us
If I could save time in a bottle

IT WAS JUST THE TWO OF US this time. It was much different from the first time - there were five of us then - and it was our first trip. We had never been there before - that first time - when we were taking our firstborn, and he was a son. The town - the campus - the buildings and people were all strange to us -

that first time.

This time it was the last one - our baby - and she is a girl - and there is *much* difference. Oh - she's been there before, this is her junior year, but it was different this time. Before she had an older brother, but now she is there alone -

it was just the two of us this time.

We drove a thousand miles together - she and I. She was excited - I was not, but you don't send your baby girl alone - in a car - for a thousand miles, no, not in this world - you just don't do that. Her mother works, her brothers work, so it was me, I don't work - I preach, and her. We left at night and we drove a thousand miles.

At first I drove - because it's mostly two lane highway through small southern towns. I drove and we talked. It was father, advisor - daughter, advisee - talk. We talked about all kinds of things - things I had planned to talk about - and it was serious. She listened patiently, agreed, acknowledged - she tried to understand. She's twenty now - she's grown - and we haven't always been friends - in fact, although we have loved each other fiercely, we have not liked each other - often.

We are too much alike to like each other.

After we talked about the serious things we fell silent. It wasn't that we didn't communicate, we just didn't talk. Words weren't enough. We rode in silence - for hundreds of miles, she dozed, I dozed, but mostly we were awake and we were very aware of each other, and what we were doing.

The town is familiar now, the buildings are like old friends. We know the instructors and administrators - we know the politics, problems and potentials. This is a good place for her - I am glad it exists. I feel good about her being here and it delights me that she is so happy here.

The past summer was hard on both of us. She did not enjoy being at home. There were no friends, no activities, her job was boring, her evenings were lonely and she was often unhappy. She tried, so did we - she really tried to be satisfied with us but the time has come - her time - and we both knew it. She said she was sorry about the summer - that she really loves us - *but,* she said - yes, dear God - *but* - It is that time. She does love us - but it is her time, and love is not enough to cover that - though it is the greatest thing of all.

It was different this time. Normally I drive back home - this time I flew, but it was the same heartbreaking as the first time. She is the last, I will not do this again - and dear God, I **want** to do this again. Her time has come - and my time too - but,

I know what time it is,
she does not.

She drove me to the airport. It was quiet and it was *small talk.* At the really important times, you can't say much anyway. I asked her not to come in and wait for my plane. I didn't think I could take that - and I hate to appear foolish in public. We parked in front of the terminal and I got out and got my bags. She got out too. We stood close and looked at each other - the look said much - it really occurred to me how much she looks like her mother - it was time - our eyes filled and then we held each other for a long time - and that said much too. *I'll be all right, Dad,* she said to reassure me. *I know,* I said, *that's not the problem - that's not it at all. You wouldn't understand - you couldn't right now. It's not your fault - it's just time.* And that's what it was, you know, I saw it so clearly - it was a cool, early September morning in 1958 - I was getting into my 54 Ford convertible and my father was standing on that old rickety wooden back porch there on Rochester Road - just watching me as I backed out of the driveway heading for college. It was *time* that he was watching and now I was watching it.

I love you, Dad, she said, *I love you too,* I said. We did not mean the same thing, but it was good and it will last -

because we do, you know.

When I walked into the terminal I found myself singing in a cracked, broken voice - Jim Croce's song,

Time In A Bottle

The words are:

If I could save time in a bottle

If words could make wishes come true

I'd save every day till eternity passes away

Just to spend them with you.

And that's what it is - it's *time*. Solomon said, *There is a time for everything.* He was right and that shouldn't surprise us. He also said that most folks main problem is, that they don't know what time it is - they're always running around in circles when it's time to stand still. God is always trying to get us to see what time it is but we are far too busy or careless or insensitive, besides -

we often do not wish to know.

You can't save time in a bottle - that's the rub - you can't. You can only know what time it is. There is a time when being a father is the most important thing you have to do. You can't postpone it. It won't wait for you - there is no *next year* in fathering. One day you wake up and they're grown and gone and you realize that you missed the only chance you're ever going to get.

Do you know what *time* it is -

in your life?

Time in A Bottle
Maybe You Can!

I FINISHED THE LAST STORY by saying that you can't save time in a bottle - maybe I was wrong. You know it's the most amazing thing how your mind works. The morning after I wrote that story down, I woke up thinking about Fred Alexander. I couldn't figure out why. I've only seen Fred two or three times in the last thirty years. I laid there in bed and puzzled over it - did I have a dream, with Fred in it, that I couldn't remember? And then it came to me, I don't know how or why,

but it came to me.

We were at Michigan Christian College and it was the spring of 1961. The school year had just ended, finals were over, dorm rooms were empty, annuals signed, cars loaded, goodbyes said - we were going home. There were seven or eight of us left, as I remember it - Wayne Baker, John Losher, Jim Began, Bill Hall, Bob Forrester, John Whitwell, Gary - something, myself, and Fred Alexander.
We were the only ones left.

We met in one of the now empty, bare, sterile dorm rooms. Fred Alexander was a school administrator of sorts and he also served as the chorus director. He and his wife, Claudette, were much loved by the students.

We met by design – one of the boys had specifically set up the meeting and had invited Fred. We met to say goodbye – in some final, official, personal way. Each of us tried to say something important – significant, to find an expression for what was in our hearts – to give vent to the love, the sorrow, the loneliness that we felt.

We were so aware of time.

We had not been aware at all. We had played football and basketball in the long fall afternoons – we had eaten in the cafeteria, gone to chapel, dated the girls, talked late at night about unimportant things, gone to Red Knapps for hamburgers, played spades and hearts, crammed for tests, bragged and fooled away endless hours canoeing on the Clinton River and visiting Yates Cider Mill – all with no consciousness of time – but we were conscious now – painfully so. The year was over – time does not need consciousness to pass – things had changed without our notice –

they would never be the same again.

The meeting was awkward – we were embarrassed – we were only boys and we were experiencing things for the first time, so we had no words. Although I was older than the other boys, I was as lost as any of them, maybe more so, because growing up had come very slowly to me.

Finally, we joined hands in a circle – and we prayed. And as we prayed we began to cry – first one – then another – finally all. It was a new experience for some of us. When we finished our prayer, we shook hands – then, awkwardly we embraced each other –

and then it was time to go.

We asked Fred if he had something to share with us. His eyes were red too – I don't think he was much used to crying either. His voice shook, but I remember what he said.

If I could have any wish right now -
I'd wish that I could take this moment
*and **put it in a jar** - and put a lid on it,*
so each of us could hold it.
And every now and then - wherever we go -
at those special times when life is cruel
*and we needed it so badly - we'd **open the jar***
and let a little bit of what is in this room out -
and we would remember the experience
of loving and being loved -
and it would make us whole again.

He may have said more, but that's what I remember. Oh, my dear brother Fred - how I need that jar today. I do remember that moment and writing about it has been just like opening the jar - I don't know -

maybe I was wrong -

Maybe you **can** save time in a bottle,
Maybe you **can** preserve the loving,
Maybe **remembering** is as good as being there,
No, you can't **go** back, but you can **be** back.
Maybe you **can** save time in a bottle.

That's the payback, fathers. That's what you get for being there - for struggling - for sacrificing - for the raising. You get precious memories and so do your children. Memories are sustaining things, they give meaning and purpose not only to the past but to the present and they bring hope for the future.

Reach up and take that jar off the shelf - open the lid slowly - careful not to let too much escape at once. Savor every aroma and draw strength for today from the blessings of the past.

Precious memories, how they linger
How they ever flood my soul
In the stillness, of the midnight
Precious sacred scenes unfold.

Mothers

MOTHERS ARE SPECIAL. The two most lasting impressions I have of my mother are first, her "thereness" – by which I mean that she was simply always there. Breakfast, lunch, supper, going to bed, getting dressed, laundry, weekends, after school, late night sickness, special occasions, coming in late – she was there. Dad spent long hours at work or was busy reading or off on errands – mother was there. She always had time for me and she was always interested in what I was doing.

The second impression, I will simply call her "faith." It was the most dominant, tenacious, unyielding, pervasive aspect of her being. When I was small I simply accepted it. Now that I have had to wrestle with doubts and fears to maintain my own faith – I marvel at hers. She read her Bible every day. I mean **every** day – not just for five minutes but for extended periods. And she didn't just read, she studied, memorized, and meditated – and she believed – yes, she believed what she read and that faith formed the foundation of her life, her love, her conversation, her relationships and her notions of right and wrong.

Her faith permeated our house.

My mother had many faults. As a child of course, I did not see her idiosyncrasies as faults – I didn't see them as idiosyncrasies either. As I grew older, her faults became more obvious to me. She had a terrible, unreasonable fear of poverty, which drove her to exhaustion trying to prevent it. It also caused her to be frugal – miserly is a better term – to a painful degree. She was extremely opinionated, and expressed her opinions with great vigor, often at the expense of other people's feelings. She had a difficult time being happy – it was almost as if she thought it was ungodly.

I reached a point in my early adulthood, where my mother's faults began to dominate my feelings toward her, and I must admit that I was impatient and even avoided her. By God's grace, many of my memories of what she had told me about her childhood returned to me, and I marvelled at how far she had come and how much better a home she had given me, than what she had had.

Today, I honor her memory. To a very large extent, I am what I am because of her. Even more than my father, my mother's faith, character and personality are reflected in my life.

When children grow up - especially sons - they think that their mothers are foolish, sentimental, overprotective and old fashioned. They find themselves saying things like, "Oh mother, for heaven's sake, I'm twenty years old," or, "yes, of course I'll be careful." Fortunately, they soon become husbands and fathers and somehow that cures them pretty quickly.

Two Notes

FOLLOWING ARE TWO notes. They are printed here exactly as I wrote them. They reveal much about my mother - and about me. The first one I wrote when I was seven or eight. I have no specific memory of the occasion, but when my mother died, I found this note among her treasures. She had saved it for thirty years - through a multitude of moves - through good times and bad -

she hung on to this note.

The second note is self explanatory. She never read it - at least not with her physical eyes. The notes say much - they contain great truths. I never got to be a better son - hopefully, I have become a better man. And that of course is what she wanted me to be - a better man. It is my prayer that you men who read this - will weep for your failures to be the sons, husbands, and fathers that you could have been. It is my prayer that you will (by God's grace) be motivated to become what you ought to be.

Dear Mother

I have come
home from camping
had a lot of fun.
I came home for a while
I got here about
20 to one I have
gone ice skating
at the pond I
will make sure
I will not get
hurt at all

John

Will be home in
hour or two

Written in the winter, either 1943 or 1944.

57

January 24, 1975
8:15 A.M.

Dear Mother,

I am on an airplane to Michigan to see you. Jary called last night to say that you had a severe stroke and that you hadn't regained consciousness.

This sickness and the thought of your impending death has given me cause to consider some things. I feel a very deep need to ask your forgiveness for my extreme selfishness in failing time and again to show proper and Christian consideration to you and your needs. I have failed to do a multitude of small things that I thought of — and knew they would please you — yet just didn't do them. I feel that you have endured more from me than anybody has a right to expect — even from a mother.

It is my prayer that if we have a future here that I will, with God's grace be a better son, and a better Christian than I have been. God has brought me very low. I praise His name for what He has shown me about myself.

John

Mother's Day

IN 1944 OUR COUNTRY WAS ENGAGED in a world war. I was seven. A member of our family had been killed at Pearl Harbor so the war was very real to us. My mother read daily newspaper accounts of death tolls and battles, won and lost. It was a frightening time.

My father worked long hours at a converted Chrysler automobile factory – now simply called, *The Tank Arsenal*. He did not get home till very late at night. Because we lived in a rural setting, my mother was often very apprehensive during his absence, she refused to go to bed until he arrived home and so we passed the time by singing. My mother would play the piano and she and my sister and I would sing. We sang, *Red River Valley, You Are My Sunshine, I've Been Working on the Railroad*, and we sang church songs too – *Sweet Hour of Prayer*, and *When We All Get To Heaven*. My father was from Arkansas and he had taught us some deep south songs like, *Old Kentucky Home, The Camptown Races*, and *Old Black Joe*.

One night, after singing long, I went to bed before my father came home. The song, *Old Black Joe* remained on my mind.

> *Gone are the days,*
> *When my heart was young and gay.*
> *Gone are my friends,*
> *From the cotton field away.*
> *Gone from the earth,*
> *To a better land I know.*
> *I hear their gentle voices calling,*
> *Old Black Joe.*
> *I'm commin', I'm commin',*
> *For my head is bending low,*
> *I hear their gentle voices calling,*
> *Old Black Joe.*

I don't know all the reasons why that song made such a profound impression me – maybe it was the war, thoughts of death – or it was the uncertainty we all felt, but my child's heart was moved. I felt so sad for Old Black Joe that I began to cry and the more I cried, the harder I cried. My mother heard me and came to my room. She sat on the bed in the dark and stroked my head and held me. She asked me what was wrong and I told her I didn't like that song about Old

Black Joe because it made me think about dead people and sad things and I thought he must have been terribly mistreated to be so sad.

She told me that there was much grief in the world and much injustice. She said that dying wasn't such a bad thing always – that sometimes it was better than living. She said that Old Black Joe wanted to be with his friends and now he was – that heaven was a nice place and that God had a very special place for Old Black Joe and his friends and they were having a good time together.

I went to sleep so happy for Old Black Joe, and loving God who was so nice to him. I was glad that Old Black Joe was having a good life there because he had had such a bad one here. I really believed what my mother told me. I trusted her completely. It was the foundation of my faith and I still believe it

to this very day.

Sometimes, like today especially, I miss her till I ache. I miss her steadfast faith in a loving God and I wish I could lay my head in her lap and she would stroke my hair and soothe my fears. I believe that God has a special place for her and that she and her friends are happy and singing with Old Black Joe and his friends.

> *For I am mindful of the sincere*
> *faith within you, which first dwelt in*
> *your grandmother, Lois, and in your*
> *mother, Eunice, and I am sure that it*
> *is in you as well.*
>
> II Timothy 1:5

Learning to Read

MY MOTHER TAUGHT ME to read – She didn't mean to – I mean she wasn't trying to, but she did. I do not know when she began the practice but I do know that from my earliest remembrances she read to me every day before my nap – except Saturday and Sunday. My father was at work and my sister at school, so we would crawl into my parents' bed and prop the pillows up against the iron posts of the bedstead – after *fluffing* them of course, what a shame that modern children don't even know the word *fluffing,* because they don't *fluff* – you can't with polyester and foam rubber – fluffing is like shaking up – we've added *microchip* to our vocabulary and deleted *fluffing,* it was a sorry exchange, and our language is the more barren. Anyway, we fluffed the pillows, nestled back into them, huddled very close to each other and she would read.

What did she read? The Bible of course – what else? It was the only book in our house. She read stories from the Bible. She was a *finger reader.* When I first read at school I read the same way, but my teacher, Miss Smoky, absolutely forbade it. I told her my mother read that way and she said it was okay for my mother but not for me. Miss Smoky was very nice – and she meant well – but I'm really glad that my mother's teacher didn't forbid her to read with her finger because if she had you see, I wouldn't have learned nearly so soon or so well and I might not have loved it so.

Oh, you may not know what a finger reader is. It's like *fluffing* I guess. A finger reader is a person who follows the words with their finger so they won't lose their place or jump to the wrong line. It makes perfectly good sense if you think about it. In schools nowadays, we're very concerned with how fast people read – if you can read a thousand words a minute that is absolutely fantastic – and it doesn't really matter if you understand the words, or enjoy them, or take the time to think about them – you must learn to read them very quickly – because there are so many of them and if you don't read quickly – my goodness – you may never read all of them. And reading all of them is terribly important, even though most of them aren't worth much.

My mother was a finger reader. Every day as she read, I would hear her voice and watch her finger as it went back and forth across the page. Of course it happened very slowly – and I didn't know I was learning to read – I honestly didn't even mean to learn – it was quite an *accident.* I began to associate what my mother was saying with the word above her finger. There are lots of *ands, thats,* and *buts* and I guess I learned those first. It was easy for an uncluttered mind to grasp that it took a long time to say, *Belshazzar* and it also took a lot of letters. The more I learned, the more fascinated I became with my mother's voice and her moving finger.

One day I corrected her. She either mispronounced or skipped a word – I don't remember which, and I corrected her. She was incredulous. *How did you know that?* she asked. I didn't know how

I knew, I just knew that the word she said wasn't the word that was above her finger. I did not know the alphabet - that would come much later in school. I didn't know phonics, I still don't, but I could tell a telephone pole from a fire hydrant and I could tell the difference between Jehu and Jerusalem. My mother asked me to read and I did it gladly - slowly, haltingly - finger under the words - with her coaching I read. Then I read with no coaching and we took turns, Mom read one day - I read the next.

When I went to school a couple of years later, Miss Smokey tried to teach me to read. I told her I could already read. I could tell it hurt her feelings, so I said I was sorry - but reading was a piece of cake - they were reading Dick and Jane and I knew Nebuchadnezzar, Jebusite, Perizzite, Shamgar and Rehoboam. I told her she could teach me math,

I was real dumb in that.

But I want you to see - that if my mother was teaching me to read - without meaning to, she was also teaching me about God, about right and wrong, about good and evil - yes, those ideas were forming in my mind - waiting for the moment when I would need them to help me to understand my growing - changing world.

She didn't mean to - any more than she meant to teach me to read. She read the Bible because she loved to read the Bible - because it had great meaning to her. If I hadn't been around she would have read it anyway, and after I went to school and didn't take naps anymore she continued to read. She only knew that it entertained me and that it was good for me in some general way.

Again, my specific point is that both teaching me to read and teaching me about God, about good and evil, and standing for the right did not come to me through lectures and sermons - although I heard plenty of them at church - they came to me through my mother's attempt to establish and strengthen her own relationship with God.

Her daily awareness of His providence –
Her constant devotion to His will –
Her love for His word, passed to me –

naturally.

Mother's Cherry Tree

MY MOTHER LOVED ALL GROWING things. We had apple trees, pear trees, a grape arbor, a rose arbor, tulips, lilacs, irises, and an annual garden. The Murdocks, who lived directly west of us, had a large cherry orchard. Although they gave us all the cherries we wanted, my mother was determined to have her own cherry tree. Accordingly, one fall we planted (I say we, because I dug the hole) a three foot sapling. Mother fertilized, watered, watched over, pampered and stroked that tree until it was a wonder it didn't die from too much attention. It was amazing how it grew, and in its second spring it actually blossomed and bore cherries – not enough to make a pie, but my mother was so proud of the accomplishment that she nearly burst. She even carried some of those cherries in her purse to show her friends.

We always shopped at the A & P grocery store in Royal Oak. Fortunately for me, just down the street was Frentz & Sons Hardware. While my mother shopped, I wandered up and down the aisles of Frentz & Sons. It was a fascinating place. Great bins of nails, rows of hinges, racks of shovels, balls of twine, smells of feed, seed, leather goods, and a hundred other items all combined to make it a whole world in itself. Inevitably, I was led to the fishing equipment, then the gun rack, and finally to the knife display case. It was a wooden cabinet with a glass door. I stood for long minutes gazing in wonder that there could be so many fine things to be had.

At the bottom of the knife case there was one item in particular which attracted me. It was a belt hatchet – just the right size for me. It had a leather case which could be strapped right onto your belt for carrying purposes. I began to pester my mother about it. One day she actually went in to look at it and I knew that my pleading was getting somewhere. It was a long process, but eventually she bought it for me.

I remember going around the yard whacking on things. It was exceedingly sharp. I whacked on old two-by-fours. I whacked an old crate apart which had been sitting behind the chicken coop, but it was all very dissatisfying. I wanted something more substantial to cut. All of the trees on our place were far too large for me to tackle with my hatchet – all except one – the cherry tree. As preposterous as this seems, the idea was probably enhanced by my school teacher telling us about George Washington cutting down the cherry tree.

Since George was quite a hero, the idea of cutting down our cherry tree was an easy step.

I guess that actually walking up and cutting it down was a little too much for me all at once, so I decided to *trim it* a little first. The result was that I left not a single limb intact. Our cherry tree was reduced to a forlorn looking, tapering rod protruding from the ground. Around its base lay a pile of limbs with the leaves looking limp and sickly.

When I stepped back to survey my work, my conscience began. You know consciences are often the most useless things. When I needed it was before I started, but it was completely silent - didn't help me a lick; never said, *John, you'd best think about this,* or *are you sure this is what you want to do?* Now, when it was too late to be of any use whatsoever, here it came - full blast. *Now look what you've done,* it cried. Pictures of my mother fertilizing and watering - her proud tones as she displayed those first cherries to all of her friends, all flooded my memory and made me feel terrible.

But, what good did it do to feel terrible
after the fact?

I put my hatchet in its case and wandered slowly into the kitchen. I had studied some on how best to approach this situation, and had decided that it would be to my best advantage to open the subject before it was discovered. *I know a little boy who cut down a cherry tree,* I piped in my most cheerful, winning voice. My mother, busily occupied, replied, *Oh, I bet I know who it was. It was George Washington.* She said it so nice and sweet that I was reassured and plunged ahead. *No, it wasn't. It was John Smith.* Right off, there was a noticeable change in both the temperature and the atmospheric pressure in the kitchen. My mother turned on me quickly, and her voice didn't have any sweetness in it, or light either, for that matter. *Did you cut down my cherry tree?* She grabbed me by my left ear (she was right handed so her grip was better), and we marched out to the scene of the crime with her nearly lifting me off of the ground - using my left ear for leverage.

I would have gone anyway.

When she saw the tree she started to cry, and since she needed both hands to dry her eyes, she turned loose of my ear, which was a great relief. It was a sad looking sight, standing there like a little flagpole, but I thought things might go a little easier for me since she was so sad and all. It didn't. She whipped me with every last limb I chopped off that tree - whipped me till the limb was just shreds of bark left

in her hand. I was afraid she was going to start on the pear tree limbs, but she finally gave out. You know, a person is mortally strong when they're aroused like that, and they also have an amazing endurance. It cheered me some to think that she was using the limbs on me
instead of the hatchet.

You know, my mother went right back to work on that cherry tree. She kept right on watering and fertilizing and caring for it. Anyone else would have given up. She willed that tree to live and it did. It grew and became a fine tree with only a few scars on its trunk -
to remind me of my folly.

Isn't it amazing how things will grow if they get the right kind of attention? I strongly suspect that there's a lot of folks around right now who were at one time near to death, like mother's cherry tree, because some thoughtless rascal started cutting on them, but now they're healthy and growing because somebody kept watering and fertilizing and loving them and they lived. In fact, I strongly suspect that's what happened to me. Today, I am healthy and strong, with only a few scars to remind me of my folly and some folks' attempts to trim me, and I stand here knowing Christ because both, He and my mother, wouldn't quit on me.
She willed me to live,
and I live as a result
of her love and determination.

Providence

MY GRANDMOTHER WAS SHORT, her face was very thin with a decidedly unhealthy yellowish pallor. Her cheekbones were high and protruding, and she wore steel-rimmed glasses. Her dresses were straight, shapeless, nondescript affairs, and I cannot remember her ever *dressing up*. Her hair was always pulled straight back into a tight ball at the back of her head and it was gray and thin. She had several teeth missing and the remaining ones were yellow and crooked. She was a little stooped, and one of her shoulders hung lower than the other, which gave her a lopsided and slanting appearance.

I do not remember ever hearing her laugh
or seeing her happy.

She lived in downtown Detroit on Seventeenth Street not far from
Michigan Avenue, which is where Briggs Stadium is, the home of
the Detroit Tigers. The appearance of her house was much like her
own. The foundation had decayed and the entire structure slanted,
tilting dangerously to one side. Inside it was always dark. She never
opened the blinds, and only one light ever burned. It hung down
by its frayed yellow cord from the cracked plaster ceiling, over the
kitchen table, where we always sat. It was a bare light bulb, with no
shade or covering.

When you entered the house you were in the living room, if such
it could be called, for no one ever lived there. It was stacked high
with an odd assortment of furniture, at least I always supposed it was
furniture, which was covered by an even more odd assortment of old
sheets and cloths. The dust lay thick upon the rotting, disintegrating
cloths and it got on your clothes and skin when you walked the
narrow, winding path from the front door to the kitchen.

I did not like to go there. It was a forbidding old place in a
forbidding old neighborhood with rude, unfriendly, suspicious
children. The slanting floors, the semi-darkness, even my grandmother herself gave off an eerie unpleasantness which made me
long for my rural home.

My grandmother drank. I knew little about it for a long time and
understood less. As I grew older, it came to my attention that she
drank a lot. My mother went to visit her frequently. I'm sure she
went with a heavy heart. She took me with her for support and for
an excuse to leave. She knew that my grandmother would upbraid
her for her lack of devotion and she would have to listen to her retell
the story of all the wrongs she had suffered at the hands of her family.
Unfortunately, it was all too true. She had been wronged. She had
been abused, cheated and lied to by those nearest her. They had
taken advantage of her age, her weakness for drink and had stolen
from her. She was bitter, cynical, and thoroughly miserable, and she
sought constantly to bring my mother into that web of misery
which was the only source of purpose she had in her old age.

As we rode the bus to my grandmother's house, which would take
hours, and as we returned, my mother would talk to me about her
childhood and about my grandmother in better days. She told the
stories in such a way that it helped me to understand all that my
grandmother had been through and the things that had made her

this way. I grew to feel very sorry for my grandmother, and I learned how circumstances can change people.

Those stories made lasting impressions on me. I remember most of them to this very day. Mother would almost always begin by telling me about how she came to this country as a little girl; about the naturalization process; then about her life on the streets of Detroit in the very early nineteen hundreds; of being placed in a foster home when her parents could not keep her; of going to work for A.T.&T. as a long distance operator; of loose, wild living and then of meeting my dad; of marriage; of my sister being born; and then it would always be the story of her faith, which was told in great detail. She obeyed the gospel the very first time she heard it, under the preaching of Jewel Norman.

As she told the story of her life, it was always in view of a great, guiding providence. Even a child could understand that she believed that God had been intimately involved in her history and that only by His grace had she been born into His family. Because she believed that so firmly, it came to me that I also was under His providential care and it gave me a peace, even as a child, and confidence which greatly altered my life.

I urge you, not only to tell your history to your children, but to tell it in such a way that God's providence is evident. Help them to see how they fit into that providence. It will provide the basis for the kind of relationship which will sustain them when troubles come.

Pancho

THEY SAY THAT DOGS TAKE ON the personalities of their owners and if that's so, old Pancho's previous owner had to be the most miserable grunt of all time. I can't remember where my mother got him, but he had short, black, curly hair and was totally irascible. He didn't like any of us - except my mother, and I never thought he really liked her, it was an act he put on so he could keep the perfect situation he had fallen into. He was mean tempered. Every time I approached him, he pulled his lips back and snarled deep in his throat.

Nobody ever petted him or spoke to him except mom. She

bought him the best food, curried and brushed his coat, fussed and made over him till the rest of us were sick. She said we were just jealous because he wouldn't take up with us - and maybe we were. I hoped he'd run off, but he was too smart for that, he knew he'd never get another ticket like the one he had, so he rode it and milked it for all it was worth, and in a dog's world, it was worth plenty.

Now that you know how I felt about Pancho, you won't be surprised at my reaction when I saw him sort of limping around behind the house and acting like he was sick. *What's the matter, you vicious old bugger, did you try to molest some little girl and get the slats kicked out of you?* He didn't pay any attention, but then he never did, so I went inside. I told my mother that Pancho was acting funny and she became very concerned. *What do you mean, funny?* she said. *I mean he didn't snarl or try to bite me when I walked by, and he was limping.*

She went outside but was back in a moment. She wanted me to go and check on him because he was in his house and wouldn't come out. I tried to coax him out, but he wouldn't come so I reached in - true to form, he tried to bite me. I jerked my hand back and told my mother that I hoped he had leprosy, the jungle rot and Asiatic flue. I said I hoped his temperature would go to about two hundred degrees and it would damage his brain so he would be more normal. I was real upset. She tried to get me to make another attempt but I wasn't having any, so we just left him to sleep it off.

When I went back that evening after supper, he was dead, *deader than a doorknob,* as we used to say - which is pretty graphic when you think about it. It would be nice to say that I was sorry and that I regretted doing mean things to him but it wouldn't be true, because I wasn't. But mother was. She cried and carried on and we all felt bad for her because she really loved Pancho in spite of all his faults.

I dug the hole, and we buried Pancho out behind the house under the apple tree. It was just the three of us, Mom, Dad, and I and we didn't say anything but she wanted us there for the burial. I looked out the window late that evening and saw my mother standing beside the grave grieving. For as long as we lived there, when evening came and I couldn't find my mom, I knew where she would be. When we moved from that house, when the last of the furniture was loaded and we were ready to go, we couldn't find her and dad said, *I know where she is,* and so did I. I can see her there yet.

She kept a picture of Pancho playing ball with her (on one of his rare *good* days) on her dresser, and for years she talked lovingly of her favorite pet.

Pancho died without a friend in the world except my mom. But that was like her. She was always picking up strays, sticking up for folks that no one else had anything good to say about. She was always ready to help people who would never be able to return the favor and even when they returned her help with meanness or betrayal, she'd go right back and help again if they needed her.

Oh, Really

WE MOVED FROM ALLEN PARK, Michigan back to Royal Oak when I was a sophomore in high school. I didn't know too many people there, but I struck up a tentative friendship with a boy who sang first tenor next to me in the acappella choir. One day we were talking before practice began – that inquisitive, casual, but probing kind of talk which ultimately determines whether your friendship rises or falls. He told me where his father worked and what an important position he held. I told him that my dad sold batteries and electrical parts for cars.

He asked if I was familiar with a certain ladies' fashion store in town, and when I said I had heard of it, he said with an air of unconcealed pride, that his mother owned that store and was responsible for its operation. Not to be outdone, I quickly related that my mother worked for Judge Arthur E. Moore. When he asked what she did, I said she was a housekeeper. He was obviously impressed by the name but he was uncertain about the term, *housekeeper*. When he inquired as to what a housekeeper did, I said that she cooked, cleaned, made beds and did laundry for them. He said, *You mean your mother is a "cleaning lady?"* His tone was slightly incredulous. I said that I guessed that was right, but I had never thought about it exactly in those terms. He turned to the boy sitting beside him and said, *Hey, John's mother is a "cleaning lady." Oh, really,* the boy responded. There was no mistaking the tone.

For the first time in my life,
I wished my mother had a different job.

It bothered me all day. It occurred to me on my way home that I had never thought of my mother as a *cleaning lady* – I thought of her, more than anything, as my mother. I thought of her work as being very necessary and useful - much more useful than a fashion shop, when it came to that. I decided that a person needed to know much more about my mother, and her work, before they were qualified to say,

Oh, really.

It was obvious to me, even then, that my friendship with those boys was going to be very limited because of my parent's occupations. I am very sorry to say that I felt the loss deeply. I had no way of knowing then that their friendship was worth about what a ladies's fashion shop was worth, almost nothing. I was ashamed of my mother's job and never ever mentioned it again to anyone, but it didn't help. There were too many other unmistakable signs about me - signs I didn't even know about and couldn't possibly cover up. I was classified - *Son of a cleaning lady* - was the sign I wore, and instead of accepting it with dignity,

I languished under its reproach.

It hurts me now that I was ever ashamed of my mother, or anything about her. I know that often, children - especially from junior high through college - are ashamed or embarrassed by some things about their parents. If they have unimportant jobs - if they wear outdated, *nerdy* clothes - if they are much overweight - if they have *old fashioned* ideas about music or morals or movies - if they drive the wrong cars or are just *out of touch,* kids have a tendency to avoid bringing friends home or wanting parents to attend school functions.

Children must be taught to look deeper - to see beyond those transitory, surface evaluations of worth. Parents must not demean other people in their children's presence on such a shallow basis. Too often, children hear their parents say,

Oh, really?

Run, Tami – Run

I HAVE A DEAR FRIEND WHO LIVES in Dallas and he has a daughter who is a very talented runner. The regional cross country championships were held in my town and he called to ask if I could pick up his wife from the airport and give her a place to stay while she was there to watch their daughter run. I was delighted to do it and so I found myself on Saturday morning witnessing the Texas Regional Cross Country Races at Mae Simmons Park. I was there providentially, having had no plans nor even thoughts about going until my friend called. I witnessed something there, a wonderful, moving thing – a thing of beauty worth telling and retelling.

It was a marvelously bright, clear, cool morning and hundreds of spectators had gathered on the hillsides to watch. They were mostly family members who had traveled hundreds of miles, in some cases, to watch just one race. I had no child running, and so I often found myself watching those who did. Their faces were intent, their eyes always picking out the only runner they were interested in, and often, when the runners were far away and could not hear their shouts of encouragement, still their lips would move, mouthing the precious, familiar names, and one other word. Sometimes they said the names audibly, but softly, as if for no ears but their own, and yet it seemed that they hoped to be heard.

Run Jimmy, they whispered urgently, *Run Tracy, Run.*

The cross country race is two miles for girls, three for boys. It is a grueling, physically and mentally exhausting run over hills and rough terrain. There were ten races that morning beginning with class 1A boys and girls and ending with class 5A boys and girls. Each race had from eighty to one hundred twenty competitors. The course ended where it began, but at times the runners were nearly a half-mile away.

As the class 5A girl's race came to a close, I watched a forty plus year old mother, wearing patent leather shoes and a skirt, carrying a purse – run the last hundred yards beside her daughter. She saw no other runners. As she ran, awkwardly, stumbling, her long dark hair coming undone and streaming out behind her, giving no thought to the spectacle she made, she cried, *Run, Tami, Run! –Run Tami, Run !* There were hundreds of people crowding in, shouting and screaming but this mother was determined to be heard. *Run, Tami, Run - Run, Tami, Run, she pleaded.* The girl had no chance to win, and the voice of her mother, whose heart was bursting with exertion and emotion, was not urging her to win.
She was urging her to finish.
The girl was in trouble. Her muscles were cramping, her breath

came in ragged gasps, her stride was broken - faltering, she was in the last stages of weariness - just before collapse. But when she heard her mother's voice, a marvelous transformation took place. She straightened, she found her balance, her bearing, her rhythm, and she finished. She crossed the finish line, turned, and collapsed into the arms of her mother.

They fell down together on the grass and they cried, and then they laughed, and they were having the best time together, like there was no one else in the world but them. *God,* I thought, *that is beautiful, thank you for letting me see that.*

As I drove away from Mae Simmons Park, I couldn't get it off my mind. A whole morning of outstanding performances had merged into a single happening. I thought of my own children and of a race they are running, a different and far more important one. A race which requires even greater stamina, courage and character. I am a **spectator** in that race also. I have helped them to train, I have pleaded - instructed - threatened - punished - prayed - praised - laughed - and cried. I have even tried to familiarize them with the course. But now the gun is up and their race has begun, and I am a **spectator**. My heart is bursting -

I do not see the other runners.

Sometimes their course takes them far from me, and yet I whisper, *Run, children, Run.* They do not hear, but there is One who does. Occasionally, they grow weary, because the race is long and demands such sacrifice - they witness hypocrisy and of course there are so many voices which call to them to quit this foolish race because they cannot win. They lose sight of their goal and they falter, stumble - and I cry,

Run, Children, Run - O God - please run.

And the last hundred yards. How I long to be there, to run beside them, *Run, Lincoln; Run, Debbie; Run, Brendan; Run, Kristen.* What if I am gone, and there is no one to whisper, to shout *Run,* in their ears? What if Satan convinces them that they are not going to win? What if his great lie - that you must beat the others - causes them to allow defeat to settle over them? What if they lose sight of the great truth - that in this race, it is **finishing** that is the victory, and that is why our Lord Jesus says at the last,

*It is **finished**.*

And the great apostle Paul says,

I have ***finished*** my course.

Oh God, hear my prayer.
When their time of doubt comes -
If they cannot hear my voice -
If I must watch from beyond

Dear Lord Jesus;
As You have run beside me -
Please run beside them -
Strengthen their knees -
That they might finish.

And dear Father,
When they cross that
   eternal finish line -
May I be there to
   welcome them home.
May we laugh and cry
   through eternity -
Praising the grace which
   gave us this victory.

Run, Tami – Run

Home

I FOUND IT MORE DIFFICULT - more challenging - to write this chapter introduction than any other. So much has been written and said about home, and while most of it is true, it is also somehow inadequate. What I write here will also be inadequate. My memories of home are varied and complex because things changed so much, but before I talk about my home, I want to ask you a series of questions.

I hope you're not in a hurry - yes I know, I was supposed to start asking questions and here I am talking more and you're very anxious to get through this introduction and get to the stories and really, you'd like to just skip this, but you paid for this book and you feel like you need to read it all - to justify the expense. Now that we have that little item out of the way and you're resigned to plowing through this, let me caution you not to read over the questions hurriedly. As you read them, put the book down and think about them - try hard to answer them honestly.

1. Could you list five memories of your home that left lasting impressions?
2. Did you like being there? Always? Almost always? Sometimes? Seldom?
3. Do you remember your parents as happy? Discontented? Worried? Ambitious? Religious?
4. What types of concerns dominated the conversation in your home? Finances? Spiritual? Politics? Job? Recreation? Community?
5. Would you say that the atmosphere of your home was Relaxed? Tense? Boring? Eventful? Fun? Strict?
6. Do you want your home to be essentially

similar or substantially different from your
parent's home?

Some of these questions you may be able to answer pretty quickly and easily. Some will take much longer and the answers will be much less definitive. You will find yourself saying, *Well, it depends on when you mean,* or *Well, sometimes it was - and sometimes...* - it is that way for me. I have memories of happy, carefree, contented times, and memories of troubled, confused and frightening times. At other times, it all seems to blend together into a type of composite hybrid, which leaves me with an appropriately obscure feeling.

We all have some ideas about what home should be. We put neat little plaques on our kitchen walls with nice little poems or sayings about home - and much of it is true, but there are those nagging discrepancies between what home *should be* and what it *is,* which trouble us. *Real* homes are like *real* lives - all mixed up with good's and bad's. It's just that in some homes the good things outweigh the bad things - and when that happens we say - *I had a great home* - of course we quickly add - *sure there were a lot of bad times,* but as we grow older, even the bad times, become part of what made home so good. When folks say that they had *bad* homes - most often they mean that the outstanding memories are bad - the good times and happy days have been overshadowed by negatives.

Most parents little realize the impact of memories on a child's mind. Lasting impressions are created by the most seemingly trivial occasions. I pray that as you read the stories in this book that you will be impressed with how my whole notion about home was the result of situations that my parents had no idea would stay with me.

Although you have little control over the specific situations that create lasting memories - you do have control over how you react to them. You also control how much time you spend together as family and **how** you spend it.

You will not make lasting impressions and create sustaining memories watching television.

Parents are always saying that they wish they had more family time. *What keeps them from it?* Is it jobs - social obligations - school activity schedules? T.V.? Are those things out of your control? - Of course not - they can be changed any time we have the courage and determination to do so.

A second consideration, in this regard, is that the time we do spend together as families is of such a poor quality or so uneventful that *family time* is a downer for the children. Parents are so physically and emotionally drained by their work and social obligations that they are irritable, detached and unenthusiastic when family time comes. The result is that the kids might prefer less family time.

I do not mean that family time is a, *thrill a minute,* ride through an amusement park – in fact, I mean the opposite. Trips to Disneyland, Sea World, or even the county fair can be cop outs for parents who try to *create* good times by spending lots of money, *artificially* entertaining their children at no personal expense. I do mean that parents must invest **themselves** in whatever direction family activity takes – that family time can and must have quiet, thoughtful, meaningful moments – that there must be *drawing together* times. You cannot artificially create that – but you can create the atmosphere of caring and sharing and *being real* – that allows it to happen.

Home

WHEN I LEFT 736 CLARK ROAD in 1947, it was the only home I had ever known. I was ten. I fought the move with every ounce of my being. I left everything I knew – all that was familiar.

My father could never find a resting place after that, so between the ages of ten and seventeen, we wandered from house to house, from town to town, job to job, – looking – looking for something that he could not define, but thought he would know if he saw it. He never saw it, or at least he never recognized it, so he died still looking. I could always tell when it was moving time – the discontent – the restlessness – unpaid bills – the job wasn't working out. It was time to move again. During those years, I had no firm notion of home.

Home was just another temporary stopping place.

When I went to Tennessee to go to college, Michigan, in some general sense, became home. My family lived there and I spent summers and holidays there. My sister and brother-in-law moved to

Flint in 1956, and eventually lived there about twenty-five years. Her home became *home* to me. That's where I spent birthdays and holidays. It's where I went when I was troubled or lonely.

After twenty-five years, they left Michigan and moved to Georgia. Their move left me lonely, depressed, empty. Mom and Dad were gone. There was no reason to ever go back. I have nothing there but memories –

Michigan is not home anymore.

Some years ago, I went back to the place on Clark Road to show my children where I was raised. The old house is there, but it is much altered. The grape arbor is gone and the great pear tree which served as my ship, my plane, my tank, which had carried me on hundreds of adventures, was gone also. The trees have grown, the chicken coop, into whose wall I smashed my sister's brand new bicycle, is gone. They have even changed the name of the road from Clark to Creston.

The swamp below our house, where I turned Pete Vincent's hogs loose, has been drained and strange people have built houses there – people who neither know nor care that their house is sitting on *my* swamp, or about me, or Pete Vincent's hogs, or the marvelous shot my father made, killing a cock pheasant there one winter evening when the swamp was frozen. You see, it was an easy shot at first, but my father's hands were so numb from the cold that he couldn't get the safety off on his gun, and the bird was out of range when he finally fired. I watched it sail, with its wings set, all the way to Eighteen Mile Road before it went down. I was sad that he had missed, but he told me he was sure he had hit the bird. I wanted badly to believe him. We walked all the way across the swamp in the gathering darkness; the freezing wind blowing fine flakes of new snow around us, and our dog, Betty, found the bird dead in a clump of marsh grass and cattails.

My father allowed me to carry the gun on the way home and I walked close to him, knowing that surely no boy had as fine a father as I did.

But, the swamp is gone, and so is my father.

During the intervening years, I have followed my father's pattern, moving from house to house, town to town, job to job. I always knew that I was looking for something. I didn't know exactly what it was, but I knew I would know it if I saw it. I have never seen it and now I know why. It is not here! I am not going to find it - it will find me. When I cross the great river and open my eyes on the other side, I will know that this is it - that I am home - that every tree, every building, every rock and blade of grass is exactly where it ought to be - where I always knew it would be, and I will say, *Why, here it is - yes, this is it exactly.*

How foolish I have been.

As Christians - and as parents - we must develop a strong sense of *home*. While it is true that we are pilgrims and strangers, it is also true that God has chosen to define *salvation* as, *the **home** of the soul*. What that means to me is that it was God's plan to create - temporary, powerful - internal notions through the physical home, in order to generate longings for that permanent place of rest -

our heavenly home.

Parents have **no greater** obligation than to fix, as firmly as possible, positive notions of home in their children so that thoughts of heaven take on real and specific meaning.

I hope you're excited about going home. I hope your enthusiasm is growing in anticipation of arriving - of being reunited - of being where you belong. Heaven, like home, is where your family is. It's where you'll spend your birthdays and holidays for the next million years or so.

Value

WE HAD A GRAPE ARBOR. Huge clusters of dark, purple, Concord grapes grew there. I was nuts about them (maybe I should say *grapes* about them). As soon as they were ripe, I would pull a whole cluster and pinch the thin skins between my thumb and forefinger, squeezing the purple juice and greenish pulpy mass inside my mouth. I could do a grape about every two seconds, I figure. But no matter how hard I tried, I couldn't even make a dent in the overall population of grapes. I would leave huge piles of skins where I had stood, but the vines looked untouched.

Before the first frost, my Mom and I would make grape juice. We'd gather bushels of grapes - pull them from the stems, wash them, sort them – getting out the unripe and the rotten, and then we'd put them in cheese cloth and crush them, collecting the beautiful, dark, clear juice in a huge pan. My memory fails me on the process from that point. There was some boiling it seems, and I remember the Ball jar preparations and opening the packages of lids and seals. A layer of paraffin wax was poured on top, then the seal, and the screw-on lid. We made quite a bit and it was very good. We kept it in the fruit cellar under the house.

During the winter and into the spring we would open a jar occasionally. My mother was very frugal by nature and she rationed the grape juice out to us in what seemed thimblefuls – every mouthful was treasured. There was no swilling it down in huge gulps, so a small glass was sipped carefully, lasting all evening.

I suppose it wasn't particularly good grape juice by today's standards. We didn't strain it too good, so there was a lot of sediment. I could never get the paraffin sealer out cleanly, so pieces of wax were always floating in it. Mother never put sugar in it – couldn't afford that, so some of it was fairly bitter. Invariably, some of it began to ferment, due to a hole in the paraffin or a lid not sealed properly. I drank it anyway. It was the highlight of every holiday, birthday, or occasion, and I felt like royalty every time I was sent to the cellar to get a jar. It seemed an eternity between the last of it and the new crop.

What made me think of this, is that I just returned from the refrigerator. Inside is a half-gallon plastic container filled with grape juice – well, it was filled, it's about half-empty now. This grape juice comes in a can, it has no sediment, it is absolutely uniform in taste, there are never pieces of paraffin in it, it never ferments. There is no picking, no sorting, crushing, or boiling, – you just add water. I just drained a sixteen ounce glass in two draughts. I hardly noticed the taste. It cost me almost nothing. I do not fear running out. Our freezer has several cans.

I pay no attention.

It's an old story, a lesson told and retold by succeeding generations of parents and teachers from the beginning of time. Its truth is ageless and bottomless. I never learn it so completely that the next time it washes over me I do not feel it fresh, as I did the time it first sobered me – the lesson of value. What makes anything have worth? It is always what I pay – what it costs – how much suffering goes into it!

My children's value to me – is in direct proportion to my investment of myself in them.

Saying Grace

It was kristen who really got me to thinking about it. We were eating lunch; Kristen, my seventeen year old; Lincoln, my twenty-three year old; and I - older than both of them put together. Judi was at school (she's old too, but we don't talk about it); Brendan, he's twenty, had gone to wheat harvest; Debbie was at work. We were sitting at the kitchen table and Lincoln said, *Well, I got to go,* and he got up, stacked his dishes, and went to the sink. *When did we stop saying, "May I be excused?"* Kristen asked? It was a half serious question, and although several days have passed, it nags at me.

When the children were small, they had to be *excused* before they could leave the table. They were not allowed to sing, to interrupt, to talk excessively, or to leave the table, except in emergencies. Virtually every meal was a family experience which began with a prayer and ended with a, *May I be excused.* Every meal was carefully planned and executed by my wife and what was prepared was eaten by all -

even the peas.

Recently, I dropped by unexpectedly at the home of a couple I had been counseling. They have serious family-marital problems. It was mealtime, except there was no meal. I mean, there was no plan - no coming together. The mother flew between the can opener, the refrigerator, the cupboard and the microwave. The oldest boy took what he wanted to the living room to watch the T.V. which was blaring away. The youngest boy roamed aimlessly around the table, stuffing his mouth full of whatever he could reach. The girl sort of came and went like a squirrel, who takes a nut and disappears, then returns for another. The mother never sat down and the father, oblivious to the turmoil, visited with me over the noise of the stereo and the T.V.

Nobody passed anything.
They did not talk to each other.
They did not say grace.

It is not for nothing that the Apostle Paul tells us that God is not the author of confusion - not in the Church, not in society, and not in the home. Rather, He is the source of order, and He expects His people to lead orderly lives. When we refuse to live according to His nature, we reap the harvest of isolation that results from confusion.

How is it possible for us to have a meaningful family relationship in the midst of chaos? How can we wonder why family members are estranged, why isolation, loneliness and depression are the rule and marriage is on the rocks? I submit that under these conditions, there is no family, because the sense of order that is necessary to define the relationships is missing. And "home" has no center of reference to guide us when we need it.

Saying grace was more important than I ever knew. It was an open, practical, personal and group acknowledgement of our need and His presence. It provided an atmosphere of order which set the tone for our time together. It was a moment of quiet, of peace, and as we joined hands we were reminded that we were one – a family – and that He was integral to our family. As we passed the potatoes and the peas, we listened to each other and learned unconsciously about what a family is. If Dad talked about his job or the men he worked with, he became more real to us. If he and Mom talked about the church, or politics, or the neighbors, our eyes were opened to a larger world and our family took its place in that world. Each of us commented on his day – specific questions were asked, information given, but more than that, ties were formed and we had family consciousness.

We came to know that we were Smiths – Fred Smiths to be exact. And that there were things that Fred Smith's did, and didn't. Being a Fred Smith meant that we did not take what was not ours or what we had not earned. We obeyed authority. We told the truth. The teacher was right. Everything comes from God. You stick up for your family. You help your neighbors when they need it. You mind your own business. You never eat without washing your hands, face, and behind your ears – I never did understand why I had to wash behind my ears, I still don't. Don't buy Fords, foreign, or vote for Democrats. We learned that:

Life is not fair.
There is no such thing as luck.
Never miss a chance to keep your mouth shut.

As Smiths we believed in certain things and not in others, and we took satisfaction in our identity. One thing I always knew, Fred Smiths always say grace before they eat, and, "May I be excused?"

My notions of home were deeply founded and well defined. I knew where home was and when I was grown and married, I knew what a home was supposed to be.

What has sustained my family is the fact that during my children's formative years I adhered to my own raising. I copied the format of my father's house. At some point we began losing that. I don't know if we could have salvaged more of it or not, maybe the price seemed too high – or it was just easier to give in to social conventions. I do know it has cost us much in terms of what we cannot replace, and sometimes we do not say grace or, *may I be excused*. Now I wonder what pattern my children will adhere to as they raise their families.

Will they say grace?
Will they say, *May I be excused?*
Will they have fixed notions about home?

Home

Home is the place where,
when you have to go there,
they have to take you in.
Robert Frost, <u>Death Of The Hired Man</u>.

I HAVE KILLED MANY RABBITS. I suspect ten thousand or more. That seems an incredible number but I have hunted them for forty years and on many occasions have killed in excess of twenty-five in a single day. It is worth noting that out of all those rabbits, I remember only one as a single incident. I shot it near Evansville, Indiana on a farm which belonged to the family of Mary Lois Branstedder (now Mary Lois Moore). I was hunting with Al Strykowski and it was a cold, overcast day with much fresh snow on the ground.

We were hunting along a brushy creek bank. The rabbit, I suppose, had been searching for food and when I came too close, he darted from his cover. He was just a shadow – seen – not seen – flitting through small trees and brush. I fired – missed, fired again and scored,

I saw him tumble.

I found the place where the shotgun pellets had made long, perfectly linear tracings through the snow; found the spot where the stricken rabbit had rolled headlong; found the tiny, perfectly round, red spots of blood soaking and spreading in the snow; found where the rabbit had righted itself and begun its floundering attempt to escape. It was obvious that its powerful rear legs were broken and the rabbit was dragging itself by its front legs - tunneling through the snow. I tracked it as best I could in the dense cover, even glimpsing it now and then,

but I could not catch it.

I ultimately tracked it to a hole in the creek bank, obviously its home. It was lying, completely exhausted - dying, within my reach. As I pulled it out, it made a single last attempt to resist by pawing with its front legs, and then it uttered what I have only heard on two subsequent occasions - a high pitched wail, a sound so shrill, so filled with despair and hopelessness - so like the forlorn cry of a mother for a lost child, so eerie and haunting that I dropped the rabbit as if I had gripped a red hot coal. It made no further move or sound and when I picked it up again, it was dead. I was so moved by the event - it made such a profound impression on me that,

I shot no more rabbits that day.

I wonder yet at the powerful, instinctive drive of the dying rabbit to get home. It had just enough strength to get there - and no more. And when it got there, it made no attempt to go further - just being there was balm in itself and if **home** could not heal, healing was not to be found. Death alone could erase its pain. And that last despairing cry - how I shudder at the hopelessness - the horror of the warning it sounded to all other rabbits.

Don't wait too long, it said,
and don't get too far away.

I remember those times when stricken, bleeding, exhausted and bewildered, I have almost instinctively sought home - and it was always there. What if I had arrived and found it gone - the family scattered, no warmth, no welcome, no forwarding address.

Home, what a holy, sacred word it is. Praise God for those who stay by the firesides - keep a light in the window, a bed with clean sheets, a good smell from the kitchen and a, *We've been waiting for you,* ready. What a noble task, a high calling of God - surely, there is some place of special recognition before the throne of the most High for those who build and sustain homes – and just as surely – and sadly, a special place, away from His presence, for those who defile and destroy them.

Home –

Don't wait too long to go back,
And don't get too far away.

Today Is My Birthday

WHEN I WAS SMALL, BIRTHDAYS were much anticipated events, especially **my** birthday. Somehow or other they have lost their flavor over the years. My mother always tried to make my birthdays special by having a party. I could invite all my friends – she would make my favorite cake – fix my favorite foods – of course there were presents – we might even have ice cream and naturally, they sang, *Happy Birthday*, and I made a wish and blew out the candles – with one breath of course, and they clapped. I felt very special on my birthday and the fact that my family celebrated it, made me know that they were glad I was born and that they wanted me. Of course I didn't think about that at the time and nobody told me that that was what it meant,

but somehow I knew it.

Back in 1989 I was flying from somewhere to somewhere, and as you know, you can't fly from somewhere to anywhere without going through Dallas or Atlanta. I had a three hour lay-over between flights in Dallas and I was desperate for entertainment. I had read on the plane until my eyes were watering, so I called home to talk to my wife. She said, *Hi honey, I'm sure glad you called, Sue is in the driveway waiting on me. I hope you have a good trip - bye.* It may not have been quite that brutal but you get the idea. The call lasted about three minutes – I had two hours and fifty seven minutes to go.

I started walking – not **to** anywhere, just ambling along. As I ambled, I began to read all of the overhead signs: Baggage Claim; Gates 3-11; Ground Transportation; Emergency Exit; Restrooms;

Barber Shop; Phones; – all with the appropriate directional arrows. Then I saw one that I hadn't seen before, it said, *Chapel*. What sort of chapel do you find in an airport? My intrigue led me to follow the arrows and about a mile and a half later I found myself in a very small, plain room about fifteen feet square. There were straight backed chairs against three of the walls and a library table in the middle with about fourteen Bibles of various sorts on top. With the exception of the back wall, which was stained glass, the room was indecorous to the point of monastic austerity.

I sat down. It was so quiet after the chaotic confusion of the terminal, that it was unnerving. I prayed for a while, then picked up several of the Bibles and read short passages from each. I noticed a plaque on the wall that said the chapel was the result of a grant from the Meadows Foundation. I don't know who they are, but I'm indebted to the Meadows for that quiet place of prayer.

Under the plaque was a guest register – like you use at a wedding or funeral and I thought that was nice so I signed my name. They had provided a space in the register for people to write down their thoughts and I wrote down that I appreciated the thoughtfulness of the folks who provided the room. You know, when I finished writing I thought, *boy, that was dumb, nobody will ever go through this book and read this.* It made me feel kind of sad because some people had written quite a bit. So, I thought **I** would read it and then it wouldn't have been a waste of time.

It was fascinating – the things people had shared on those pages – I'm sure they believed no one would ever see it, and if they did it wouldn't matter. Most of what was written showed the unmistakable signs of sin – loneliness, grief, lostness and frustration with life. There was this one in particular: It said,

> *Today is my birthday. I am stranded here alone.*
> *God help me to get home - and help them to want me.*
>> I wonder if he got home?
>> I wonder if they wanted him
>> when he got there?
>> Isn't that what we all want –
>> to get home?
>> And isn't that what you want –
>> to be wanted?

Home is where you're wanted – it's where they celebrate your birthday to tell you that you're special. Home, here on earth, is the preview you get of the welcome celebration that God has planned for you when you cross the great river. When you get to the other side, you will see your birthday cake – with just one giant candle on it. The angelic host will join with the redeemed in a celestial rendition of *happy birthday*, and then you get to blow out the candle – with one breath of course – the clapping will be deafening – and then you will realize that all the things you ever wished, have come true – that you are finally and forever home – and that you are wanted. There will be a great voice – like the sound of many waters – and it will say:

WELCOME HOME - TODAY IS YOUR BIRTHDAY.

Going to Heaven

IT WAS CHRISTMAS, 1987. It's funny how thoughts – ideas come to your mind, often totally unbidden, and under the most ordinary circumstances.

I had been hunting in West Texas. It was cold – very windy – what else would it be in West Texas – and we had had a very successful hunting trip – the boys and I. We got home after dark and I was in the utility room cleaning pheasants. Like the wind in West Texas, some things never change. It's true, I had killed, **nearly** all the birds, but I had cleaned, **all** of them. Where were my boys – their enthusiasm for hunting never did extend to cleaning the game and so as soon as we hit the driveway they had very **important** plans – in this case, showers and wrapping presents.

I was alone in the utility room, but sounds of activities in the other parts of the house drifted in. I don't know how long it was before I became conscious of the symphonic blending. In the living room Kristen was playing, *Moonlight Sonata,* in the family room Judi was putting ornaments on the tree and the boys were giving her advice, while they wrapped presents.

They were laughing and talking.

There were good smells coming from the kitchen and I was overwhelmed by an unparalleled feeling of wholeness – completeness, *this is home,* I thought, which was coupled with some sadness because I knew it was passing away –

I cannot hold it.

Going to heaven became so important to me at that moment. I thought – *Dear God, I must not lose this.* I don't think I'll clean pheasants there – somehow the idea of killing anything doesn't click with my concept of a home with God, but I don't have any problems imagining that Kris will play, *Moonlight Sonata* and I'm sure we'll continue to wrap presents, sing, *Silent Night,* and celebrate the birth of our Lord.

Heaven is being able to hold those precious moments of wholeness forever. It is our,

eternal home.

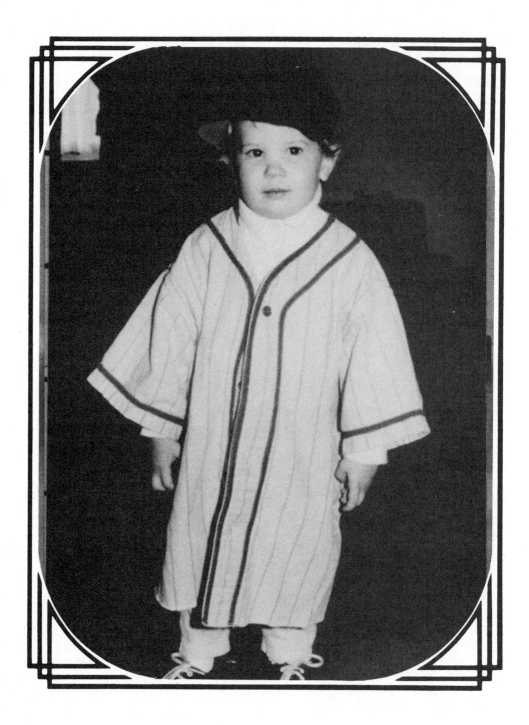

The Age of Accountability

WHEN YOU'RE A PREACHER AND some lady sort of edges you off to the side after church on Sunday morning, and then she says - very secretively - *could you come by our house this week and visit with my husband and me,* you know it's serious. Sometimes though, they fool you. You think for sure that it's marital problems and you're very apprehensive when you arrive. But when the preliminaries are over and they tell you that their ten year old daughter has been asking about being baptized - you sort of breath a sigh of relief. But then they start asking you about how old you have to be and how much you have to understand - and it's almost as bad as marital problems.

The question is about accountability. When does a person become responsible for their conduct? When does sin become a spiritual reality? We try to remember when it happened for us - when the *magic moment* arrived when we **knew**. We all know that it happens - that there was a time of *innocence* and a time of *sin-consciousness,* but when does it happen? When do we cross the line? What combination of the ingredients of age, experience, knowledge, awareness, physical maturity, and sensual sensitivity are required? Is it a moment of revelation? Is it a process?

What are the ingredients of accountability?

By accountability, I mean an awakening moral consciousness. A consciousness that has a spiritual and emotional quality inherent in it. A consciousness which recognizes those universal truths that define what it means to be human and to be responsible. An accountable person is one who not only is aware of the facts of code violations - they are aware of both the internal and external implications and have a **sense** of wrongdoing.

I heard a little story recently which may serve my point well. A mother, who was working in the kitchen, heard a piercing scream of agony from her five year old son who was playing in the bedroom with his two year old sister. When the mother went to investigate, she found that the sister, indignant over some sense of unfair play, had grabbed her brother's hair in both fists and was pulling with all her might. The mother, with much difficulty, finally succeeded in prying the little girl's death grip loose. The brother insisted that she be punished for her actions. The mother very carefully explained that the sister was so young that she didn't know that pulling someone's hair hurt and because of her innocence, she wouldn't be punished. The brother was skeptical. No sooner had the mother returned to the kitchen, when she heard another piercing wail from the bedroom. When she asked her son what had happened he said, *"she knows now."*

My point would be that there is a wide difference, even now, in what the sister knows and understands – what the brother knows and understands – and what the mother knows and understands about pulling hair and pain. Those levels of understanding each have a corresponding level of accountability.

C.S. Lewis said that he remembered the exact moment, the time, the place, and the circumstances of his coming of age and I suspect that most of us could, if we really probed our past. I know when I became accountable. I do not say that I knew it then – I had no past to judge it against and so I only knew that something had changed. I do not say that accountability came upon me full blown, like a dark cloud upon a clear sky. I do say that this was the twilight, the realization that a shadow had fallen across the clear, sunlit skies of my youth and innocence. I do say that after this incident nothing was ever the same – even though there were sunny days and happy ones – there were always vague shadows around the edges.

It seems critical to me that parents be sensitive to the tell-tale signs of budding maturity. Nearly everything changes during that transition from the innocence of childhood to the accountability of adulthood – including parental roles. Parents must be involved enough in their children's lives to be aware that an extremely tenuous and painful time is near, when character and personality take on a more permanent form.

Parenting takes a sharp turn at this point. What once was humorous is now serious. What once was serious is now humorous. What once was punished severely and spontaneously is now discussed. Hormonal and attitudinal changes leave a child totally bewildered by their own behavior. It is a time of emotional upheaval which questions everything, believes anything, remembers nothing and is always changing.

> They laugh or cry,
> not knowing –
> or caring,
> how or why.

Innocence Lost

PICTURE A STREET; AH, NO, picture two streets running parallel. Between them is an alley. Now, on either side of this alley, facing opposite directions, are two rows of houses. Have you got that? But, now here's the hard part. One of the houses is missing. That space, where the house is missing, is called a - vacant - lot, because, dearly beloved,

it has no house.

This vacant lot has become a playground for all the neighborhood children. Tag, hide and seek, kick the can, fox and goose and yes, even the national pastime, baseball, are all played upon this lot.

One fine fall afternoon about ten boys are gathered for a baseball game. You must see them. They range in age from nine to thirteen. They wear old black sneakers or are barefoot. Their T-shirts are dirty from the days' play and their blue jeans (either it was before the advent of Levi's, or we couldn't afford them) are worn, patched, or out at the knees. Their equipment consists of a single baseball, whose cover has long since disappeared and has been replaced by black electrical tape wound carefully round and round the strings of the ball. There is one bat, broken. It has three wood screws holding it together and it too is taped. The bases are either newspapers or rags held in place by rocks. Pitcher's hands are out and so is right field.

The game was hotly contested, the lead had see-sawed back and forth. No major league contest was ever played with more intensity. I was pitching. My friend, David Moody, a year and half younger than I, was on the other team. David was not a very good player, but now he was at bat.

He hadn't been on base all day. He had struck out, popped up, hit to right field or had found some new, creative way to make an out. As I said, he was my friend. We had grown up together. His folks and mine had gone to church together time out of mind. They even went to dinner and played pinochle together. His older sisters Audrey and Faye, were my sister's best friends.

Although the game was close, my team was ahead and I felt very benevolent toward David. I gave him a nice soft pitch right down the middle. David promptly took advantage of my kindness and smacked the ball across the street, right into Mrs. Owen's rose bushes. He got all the way to second base. Maybe that's where the trouble started. I was miffed because,

he took advantage of my generosity.

A couple of plays later, another boy got a hit and David decided to further impress his teammates and score. It was a mistake. He was a very slow runner. My job as pitcher was to cover home plate. I had the ball, waiting to tag him out, fifteen feet before he ever got there. He knew he didn't stand a chance, but he decided to try the only option left to him. He charged me, which was another mistake. I was a whole head taller, thirty pounds heavier, and I saw him coming. Like I said, I guess it started when he hit my pitch so hard. I had the ball in my glove and when he dove at me, head first, I just stepped back and as he flew by, I hit him right in the face with my glove.

It sort of stunned him at first, but I could tell he was real upset. Everybody hooting at him didn't help, but he made another mistake, worse than the first two. He decided to fight. I just made fun of it at first. When he tried to hit me, I just ducked or warded off his blows. He really got mad then. I guess he sort of went crazy and I couldn't stop him from hitting me some and I started to get upset myself. I pleaded with him to stop but he was like a human tornado. Finally, he hit me right on my ear and I got mad, really mad. I hit him on the nose and knocked him down. Then I jumped on him, pinned his arms to the ground with my knees and proceeded to slap his face with my open hand. Back and forth, back of my hand, palm of my hand, I slapped him. The other boys had made a circle around us and were yelling encouragement to *both* of us –

which wasn't much help to *either* of us.

When I began to come to myself. When the light of reason began to filter through my red brain, I looked down and saw the face of my friend, David Moody. It was covered with blood from his nose and mouth. I was absolutely horrified by what I was doing. It was against everything I had ever been taught. I was not by nature a bully and normally avoided fights of any kind. I didn't even like to watch.

I jumped up and I began to run. I raced down the alley into an intersecting alley, down it to the street, across the street and into another vacant lot which was across from my house. I was so overcome by the course of events that I knelt there and began to cry.

I hadn't realized that David had been following me. Bent on vengeance, he now came to where I was and found me crying. He put his arms around me and he too began to cry as though his heart would break.

Picture it if you will, two boys, one eleven, the other thirteen, arms around each other, crying in a vacant lot. Their first real dawning consciousness of wrongdoing, of having violated some sacred injunction. True to their teaching, their heritage, they begged forgiveness. They made a pact, as boys will, to ever be friends and to never allow anything to separate them.

The pact worked. They never fought again or even had cross words. I'm sorry to say that it wasn't due to their fidelity or their characters. David Moody died about a month later in a drowning accident. I remember his funeral and I remember thinking when the preacher was talking that he didn't know David very well and I wished they would let me talk because I could have told them something that would have made their hearts glad. I rejoice today that David and I parted forgiven.

At some point we all come to the realization of a need for forgiveness - that something is terribly wrong - that some ancient code has been violated and that violation somehow leaves us condemned - convicted - I know that I will never be totally at ease again - that feeling, sometimes sharp and clear - sometimes dull - remote, will not leave me. I can be forgiven but,

I will never again be innocent.

Accountability has to do with a loss of innocence, a loss which at first puzzles and confuses us - much like those first, early questions about the origin of babies, which are easily warded off - but keep returning with greater curiosity and less satisfaction. That initial loss of innocence leads us to ever more intense losses - to the discovery of evil and its mastery over our better intentions. Loss of innocence is always tied to an important event - I do not mean earth shattering

– but important to the child. It could be a death, even of a pet – the birth of a brother or sister – a storm – a dream – or a physical confrontation with some moral overtones. The search for recovery, for peace, ultimately for a return to the unbounded joy of innocence leads us ever – like the quest for the Holy Grail – back to Eden and to God.

The loss of innocence does not come once and disappear. Accountability is an on-going process and the pain and confusion which result from that initial loss are only the opening pages of a book about life which draws us ever more deeply into a seemingly unfathomable mystery.

My accountability began on a vacant lot, playing baseball, but it certainly did not end there. Oh no, and it has not ended yet.

The following stories trace a pattern of growing awareness – of increased accountability. Each event took me further down the road of realization – each one was yet another hesitating but unretraceable step toward the darkness –

that lostness brings.

Awareness

ONE DAY, RIGHT AFTER SCHOOL, I was on the playground with some of my friends, just fooling around. Mr. Dykstra, our principal, came out and began moving in our direction. It made us a little uneasy because we didn't know him too well. I knew him better than the other kids because I was a safety patrol.

When he got up close, he spoke to all of us at first – just general kinds of talk about school. Then he began talking just to me. He walked as he talked, and he led me away from my friends – sort of separating me from the flock like a sheep dog does with sheep.

When we were out of hearing distance of my friends, he began to talk to me about my clothes. He pointed out that my pants were out at the knees; there was a button missing from my shirt; and I had a hole in one elbow. I didn't believe him at first, but when I looked, sure enough, he was right. He told me I should wear nicer clothes to school, especially since I was a safety patrol.

It bothered me.

I didn't go home in tears or anything, but it was the beginning of something. I saw that my clothes were worse than the other kids. I had never noticed that before and it hadn't mattered. Now, I did notice it, and it did matter. In fact, it mattered very much and every day it mattered more.

A cloud passed over my life.

The principal did me a great favor. He made me notice something I needed to notice. He wasn't harsh, in fact, he was very kind. He brought pain into my life, that's true, but it was a *growing pain*, an awareness of my condition that needed to be recognized.

Parents need to call their children's attention to things that they are ignorant of; the cutting things they say; the prejudice they express; the selfishness which motivates even some of their good deeds.

Did you know you hurt your grandmother's feelings today?
Did you know that because you were late, everyone
else had to wait?
Did you know they were counting on you to do that?

And honestly, often they won't believe it, but when they look, sure enough, it's true, and now it matters and they are responsible for their awareness. Good parents are not unkind, or harsh, but they will be heard, and hearing them creates awareness. It is that very awareness which is their children's –

salvation from selfishness.

Selfishness

MY FATHER WAS A SPECTACULARLY poor manager of money. When I was about twelve, we suffered financial reverses so severe that we had to move to a *cabin* in a rather run down trailer court. I think it had four extremely small rooms. I didn't mind, in fact, I hardly noticed. My life went on about the same. I was in those last pre-puberty months when life is so amazingly simple and beautiful. I played baseball till dark, roamed the neighborhood, read comic books, ate, slept, went to school, and whistled my way through every day.

Life was good.

My sister was six years older – a senior in high school. I didn't know much about her and I knew nothing of her world. I would know soon enough. She was often unhappy – I knew that. We quarreled some, but never so much as we had before. She was out of my league. When we disagreed, she would just sigh and shake her head like a grown-up. When she was home she studied hard, listened to her radio, helped with the dishes and the housework, but she never talked much and to my twelve year old mind, she was hopelessly dull. There seemed to be a certain wistfulness of sadness settling over her, which made her even more disagreeable to me, because I couldn't understand why anybody should be unhappy when I wasn't. There were a few times when her face showed signs of recent tears, but I had no concept of the anguish which results from humiliation and loneliness, so I thought I must be mistaken. I didn't understand her and wasn't concerned enough to try.

I began to overhear talk about the senior prom. I could tell it was very important to her. I couldn't imagine why. I learned that a boy – who I much admired – from church had asked her to go. I didn't understand that either, I mean, what did he see in my sister? There was much fussing around the house. She needed a dress, which we couldn't afford, and there was some theological discussion about the propriety of going to a dance, which perplexed me greatly.

Prom night came. After supper – I couldn't help but notice that my sister didn't eat at all – we straightened up the house again. There was hardly anything to straighten, but I went along. She also asked me to change my clothes and to be on my best behavior, which was a bit much, but she was so earnest, so serious, that I complied with only minimal griping. She went to her bedroom to dress and I buried myself in a comic book. My dad read the newspaper –

and time passed.

Suddenly, there was a knock at the door. My dad explained that it was Jary's date. When he came in, I thought I had never seen anybody so handsome. He looked like a prince. And then my sister came out – I simply couldn't believe it, I was dumbfounded. She had on this white formal dress which contrasted marvelously with her long dark hair. She was beautiful! I mean, well, she was beautiful, and I understood why he had asked her. This was my sister – she lived in this house with me – we had grown up together. I hadn't looked at her in five years, and now – there she was –

a lady.

Something about her – and him – standing there together made me see my surroundings for the first time. Our *house* was shabby, pitiful, small and mean. It smelled of rotting wood and food cooked with too much grease. It was ill-furnished with an odd assortment of tattered, scratched chairs and a sofa with covers to hide the stains and the worn places. It reeked of low class poverty – which was okay for a kid like me – but it was no place for a lady like her. I was embarrassed for her and I thought,

She deserves better than this.

I believe it was my first totally unselfish thought – a giant step on the road to maturity, but now I was troubled, because now,

I was accountable.

Puberty

TEACHING JUNIOR HIGH FOR seven years led me to two inescapable conclusions. First, when junior high teachers die – they go straight to heaven – no looking in record books, no questions, no waiting in line, they don't even go to paradise first.
Saint Peter says:

"You look like a junior high teacher."
"How did you know?"
"Oh, by your age first, junior high teachers get here younger than the others. Second, by the look of relief on your face before you even found out where you were going. And third, by the way you looked around frantically to see if any of your students were here."
"Well you're right, I am a junior high teacher."
"Michael, send this one straight through to the gold room."

It's that simple. No amount of bad living or bad ideas will keep a junior high teacher from the pearly gates. It's a better guarantee than martyrdom – I mean like being burned at the stake – although it's very similar. The only difference is that junior high teachers get slow roasted and hung out to dry every day.

My second conclusion was that it is a big mistake to take a junior high school student seriously in the area of academics. It is a great waste of time and money to try to teach junior high kids anything – you see, their brains are not in a learning mode. When puberty sets in, a kid's brain disengages or goes into reverse and the result is that it gets stuck in one groove - **reproduction**. You can teach them anything that has to do with reproduction - if you can relate nouns and verbs, history, and photosynthesis to reproduction - they will eat it up - if you can't,

forget it.

This is the time of "best friends" and "tru luv 4 ever" – for the first of many times. It can't be avoided - it has to happen. It's the price parents pay for the sins of their youth. The only consolation I have for you is that it passes - it takes about five years, actual time, and about twenty five years off your life expectancy –

but it passes.

Love

NOTHING TESTS PARENTAL patience and skill more than the heady, bewildering experience of falling in love. It is the final act in losing innocence. Guiding a child through the emotional whirlwinds of "erotica," demands a type of sensitivity that will tap every parental resource. Because I had taught junior high school for so many years, I dreaded this time in my children's lives far more than even their learning to drive. The emotional roller coaster of exhilaration and pain - the wild, unreasonable happiness - the "cloud nine" syndrome which causes complete short term memory failure - when they can't find their room, either don't have the time or desire to eat, or, don't have the time or desire to do anything but eat, talk endlessly on the phone about absolutely nothing - then forget to hang it up - and believe everything they hear, except when their parents or –

anyone over thirty is talking.

It is inconceivable to an early teen that their stodgy, outdated progenitors ever entertained romantic notions. Dad is bald and drives a stationwagon, mom is gray, overweight and out of touch. They are both hopelessly dull - how could they possibly know anything about palpitations of the heart? That is why this time is marked with so many exasperated, "Oh how could you possibly

understands."Your major task is to first convince them that you do - not by saying you do - but by finding opportunities to tell them about that time in your life. And you must be honest about it.

Nobody is ever prepared for falling in love. How could you be? The experience comes full blown upon us with no warning. I advise parents that a good sense of humor is invaluable. I do not mean that you should make fun of, or belittle the seriousness of your child's feelings. I only mean that humor can add balance to the fleeting and ever changing emotions they undergo.

As long as things go well, in boy-girl relationships, parents play a relatively minor role. The inevitable breaking up, and the devastation that follows is very real and nearly always brings a parent into the picture. There is no better indicator of parental failure than a child consistently taking their heartaches to others.

Losing innocence, and particularly falling in love, provide critical times for bonding parents and children. It only comes once - don't miss it. It is also a critical stage in spiritual development - a time when prayer and providence become practical and,

a personal awareness of God,

becomes-

a reality.

Martha, Martha

IT WAS HER EIGHTH GRADE year, and she was painfully aware of herself - her body, her hair, even the way she walked. She was not a beautiful girl. Her face was clear, with a sprinkling of freckles, her eyes were bright, she had a laughing mouth, but she was not allowed to wear much makeup and fortune had not blessed her with that special, though ill-defined, structure of bone and flesh that we call beauty. She was on the thin side, gangly perhaps, would be an apt description. Her legs were long, her arms too, but there were already those indications of a coming grace.

Because I had taught several years at this level, I knew most of the social goings on. I knew there was a certain boy whom she wished would "notice" her. It was an almost sacred subject and she flared noticeably if any hint of such an interest was mentioned.

Unfortunately, she had set her affections on one, who in my opinion, was totally unworthy of her, and also one who I knew hadn't the slightest interest in a girl who was quiet and totally lacking in that type of glitter appeal which characterizes the junior high jet set. He was one of those boys who achieves full physical maturity at fourteen. He had broad shoulders, dark, curly hair, a dark complexion, white, even teeth and a dazzling smile. Street-wise, cocky, reasonably intelligent – in a sort of animalistic way – and fully cognizant of his charms, he was the epitome of the junior high idol – the kind of face that appeared on the posters pasted inside of every girl's locker in school.

I understood – I understood then and I understand now. It is a predestined thing, ordained in the Garden of Eden, and integrated into man's emotional circuitry. "You must at some time in your life, break your heart over the unattainable, the inaccessible, and yes – the unworthy

– only then can you become a complete person."

I was on lunch hour playground duty, standing by one of the buildings surrounded by a chaotic mob of laughing, teasing, milling juveniles. I noticed her sideways glance from outside the ring where she stood alone. I knew she wanted to talk to me, so I began moving and sending the others away. When they were gone she approached, slowly, head down, shoes scuffing the sand. I could see that she was distraught. When she got close enough, she threw her arms around me, buried her face in my chest and sobbed as though her heart would break. When she finally gained control, she looked up, straight into my eyes and said, "Mr. Smith, am I pretty?" At that moment – with her eyelashes still wet from the tears, with the intensity of agony written in her eyes, with her cheeks flushed with honest emotion, I could have honestly said, "yes," but that was not the question –

and that was not the answer.

Her classmates had found out her love interest and had been teasing her. Junior high kids can be brutal and totally without compassion. What an infinity of longing lay behind her question. In our culture it is one of the ultimate inquiries. I didn't know what to say. My answer was important to her and she trusted me so I must be truthful. I knew that I mustn't throw out some meaningless tripe – some evasive jargon that would evade the question and give hope where there was none.

No, Jeanine, you're not pretty, at least not yet,
and not as you mean it , but we need to talk
about it. I have something to share with you
that is more important than being pretty,
although I know that's very important to you right now.

We walked to the chorus room, which I knew was empty, and into my office there. I let her cry for a while and encouraged her to talk about her feelings. I knew I needed to assure her of my love and the reality of her pain. I also knew that I needed to shift her focus away from herself and the present situation. First I shared with her a story from my own junior high experience (the next story in this section) and then I took out a New Testament that I kept there and read the following passage.

Martha, Martha, you are worried and bothered about
so many things, but only a few things are necessary,
really - only one. For Mary has chosen the good part,
which shall not be taken away from her.

Yes, I shared this passage with this fourteen year old girl and even at her age, I think she understood the compassion and sympathy of our Lord and what He was trying to say. I wondered, while we talked, why she wasn't sharing this with her parents. Did she not trust them? Did they never seem to have the time? I doubt if her folks ever knew her longings, if not, they robbed themselves of one of the most important moments in their daughter's life - it passed-
      and they weren't part of it.
    I wonder now where she is, that young lady, now grown, probably with daughters of her own. I wonder if she remembers that time, and if she shares it with her little girls? I wonder what kind of mother she is and I wonder if she has gained a greater understanding of the One who

shared His life with us?

Billy's Team

BILLY HICKS WAS THE EPITOME of all the idols ever imagined by a junior high boy, he was everything we wanted to be. He was a head taller than the rest of us, he was muscular, amazingly fast on his feet, agile - by far the best athlete in school - and so strong that no one ever thought of challenging him. In addition he was very good looking. He had beautiful long blond hair that curled all over his head and his complexion was absolutely flawless - no traces of acne or chicken pox scars anywhere. His features were sharply defined - he might have modelled for a portrait of a Greek god.

He had one other attribute that needs mentioning. You might think that these qualities would have made him arrogant, vain, or most likely, a bully. He wasn't. Billy was as mild mannered, as easy going, as good natured as a Saint Bernard pup.

And when it came to girls - Billy had a way with them. They flocked around him, pleading for just a little of his attention, and Billy gave it to them - all of them. He was so at ease - laughing, teasing, complimenting and making every one of them think that she was special.

If he had a flaw, it was that he was a very poor student. Somewhere along the course of his educational career he had been held back and I never ceased to be amazed at his lack of knowledge about history or his inability to fathom the simplest concepts in math. He had no notion where Central America was or what congress was, and nouns and verbs were a mystery to him. His academic failures did nothing to diminish him in our eyes. We covered for him, constantly came to his aid, but it never bothered Billy not to know.

Even the teachers loved Billy.

Although I loved Billy, idolized him, tagged along behind him everywhere and basked in the sunlight of those who seemed to occupy a special place in his "inner circle," I was frustrated by him. Those junior high years are so critical. I was so sensitive, so aware of myself, trying to figure out who I was and beginning to notice girls for the first time. I had never understood why God had made girls before - they were the silliest and most useless things in creation - except my mother of course, but then she wasn't a girl. But I could never think of anything to say to a girl - and now I wanted badly to say something, but I just stood there, hands in pockets, head down, embarrassed and speechless.

I was also trying to establish myself as a budding athlete – to find my own place in the arena – all of the questions, the frustrations – the bewildering incomprehensibilities – they were all present in me, all at once – and Billy – well, Billy somehow stood squarely between me and the answers.

We attended a large junior high in Royal Oak Michigan. There was only one other junior high in the area so we played intramural sports. The teams were poorly supervised and for the most part were left to the discretion of the boys. Everybody wanted to be on Billy's team. There were only two teams actually – Billy's team and the "other team." Since I was the second or third best athlete, I could never be on Billy's team, I had to select the "other team," it was never, "my team," not "John's" team, just the "other" team.

When we picked teams, the boys would beg me not to select them. They would try to hide behind each other when it was my turn to pick. If I did select them, they hated me because nobody could beat Billy's team – no matter what sport we played. Billy simply could not lose, it was unthinkable. Even if I had the best all around team, which often happened because Billy didn't care much who he picked – it didn't matter. Take a boy who was minimally talented, place him on Billy's team and he would hit home runs, make spectacular pass receptions in football, and sink long jump shots in basketball. Boys who were normally good athletes – on the "other" team – could do nothing right.

Billy made the difference.

And I wanted to win; I needed to win; It was an obsession with me. Only God knows how hard I tried to beat Billy. My heart ached with it. I laid awake at night, scheming of ways to win and dreaming of what it would be like to win – just once. I broke my heart trying to win.

It couldn't be done.

I also wanted to be on Billy's team. I honestly would have given much to be less talented so I could stand among the throng and plead to be picked when it was Billy's turn, because winning meant to be on Billy's team. It could not be – the pattern was set – I must always stand on the other side and pick the losing team.

My eighth grade year passed slowly, painfully, and we moved on to high school. Eventually Billy passed out of my life. He dropped out of school his sophomore year when his bountiful good nature and warm personality were no longer sufficient to pass his subjects.

There are three ideas which come to me from that time. The first is how desperately parents need to be sensitive to those junior high years and to be understanding toward the pain, frustration, and bewilderment which lies behind the masked faces that come home from school. Those faces that - when asked how things went at school - always avert themselves from the questioner and say, "oh fine." I never talked to my folks about Billy. They didn't know that he existed. I didn't know how to do it, and I had no hope that they would understand. I'm sure they often wondered what was wrong when I came home from school - went straight to my room - and did not appear again until called for supper. I wanted to talk about it - I needed to talk about it - but my parents never shared their experiences from those years,

so I bore my pain alone.

The second idea is that Billy made the difference - he really did. Just knowing they were on Billy's team transformed those weak and mediocre boys. Not only did they perform well - they were willing to reach out - to try what they would never have tried without him. Oh, how parents need to provide an incentive to their children by showing them that Jesus makes the difference in our lives. Knowing Jesus and being on His team can and will transform us. Not only can we perform far beyond our expectations - we can reach for new horizons both spiritually and physically, knowing that on His team we cannot fail.

We can lose - but we cannot fail.

The third idea is that even as adults we want to win. Share with your children that your heart still aches with it, even in the same areas. But show them that beyond that, you have another longing which runs far deeper - a longing to be wanted and to belong. We all want to win in life - to feel that we matter - that our lives have value and purpose. As children of God, born again into His family, we have the thrill of victory - a victory of such far reaching consequences that all incidental losses are swallowed up. God has chosen us to be on His team - and that's even better than being on-

Billy's team.

Oh Very Young

Oh very young, what will you leave us this time?

IT WAS VERY LATE – ACTUALLY early in the morning – but long before dawn, when I heard the phone ring. He answered, I heard him talking and eventually I went back to sleep. Some time later I was awakened by his voice. He was at my door, his body framed by the light in the hallway, and he was calling to me, *Dad? - Dad? - Yes,* I said, *I hate to wake you up, but I need to talk to you.* He came and sat on the edge of my bed but he couldn't speak. His entire body was racked with such devastation that he trembled. I rolled over and sat beside him, putting my arms around him and pressing him to me like I had when he was a child.

He did not want to cry, he fought it with every ounce of strength he had. He was, he thought, too old to cry, too accomplished, too educated and sophisticated. His body convulsed with the struggle, he tried to speak – and then he cried. It was like the sudden breaking of a dam. He cried because life had been cruel and had delivered a crushing blow at a most inopportune moment. He said he had fallen in love – and he had, but she had not.

He cried because he was only a boy –

a boy who was trying, to become a man.

We sat on the edge of the bed and he tried to tell me how much he hurt – how sick he was. I understood, I had been sick too. We talked of suffering and its redemptive value. I told him that suffering and grieving were great gifts – giant steps in the process of knowing God. It was true, but I don't think he heard and if he did, he could not place this truth in the context of his grief. I cautioned him that grieving for personal loss was a necessary step toward grieving for the suffering of others. Self centered suffering is necessary – it must always come first, but it can become a type of greed or self pity, if it does not lead us to suffer for others – to understand their heartaches and woes.

I also tried to tell him that when he had learned to suffer for others, his own sufferings would diminish, not because they were less or fewer, but because he would not take them into account. I even tried to share with him what I had learned, first from the Bible and David's grief over his rebellious son Absolom, but Dostoevsky had phrased it for me in <u>The Brothers Karamazov,</u>

God, help me to be worthy of my sufferings.

That is an idea worth reaching for.

I told him that it would pass – though he did not believe me – that time would leave only a small scar to remind him of the step he had taken. I also hoped that he would somehow know that he was a better man in his grief than he had ever been in his joy – that he was far closer to the springs of life, the essence of fleshly experience here, than he would ever be anywhere else – that he was closer to the heart of love, of God Himself, than he had ever been before.

He said that he needed to go to her – that he needed to see her face and look in her eyes when she said the words. She was a thousand miles away. I tried at first to dissuade him, telling him how foolish it was – that he needed to accept it and go on with his life – and then – I remembered – I remembered another girl and another time and I told him to go – to go quickly, immediately – to not rest until he had satisfied his need. I helped him pack and he left.

It was still dark.

Thirty-six hours later, he was back. He had seen her – they had talked. Nothing was changed – oh, yes – my son was changed – he would never be the same –

awareness was upon him.

The years have passed and my son is now a man. Much has happened to both of us since that night, but he has never forgotten. I felt then that our talk had made little impact or impression – time has proved me wrong. I praise God for that time and for the bond that was made that night.

Oh very young, what will you leave us this time?
You're only dancing on the earth for a short while,
And though your dreams may toss and turn you now,
they will vanish away like a summer's dew.
And though you want them to last forever
You know they never will,
And the patches make the goodbyes harder still.

Cat Stevens

She's All Right

IT NEARLY ALWAYS COMES at night, and most of the time it's very late. I had been asleep for some time when the phone rang. I fumbled clumsily in the dark for the receiver, knocking the kleenex box onto the floor – then tipping the lamp over. Muttering under my breath that if this was a wrong number or a solicitation of some sort – somebody was going to get an earful – I finally found the phone and mumbled a very unfriendly, *hello*. There was that pregnant silence that creates apprehension and then this sound;

Dad!

Just the one word – and then silence again – I was fully awake.

Dad!

No more was said, but my reply was instantaneous.

Kris? - What's wrong?

The next sound that I heard is known to every parent – every person. From the cradle to the grave – it is the universal cure for heartbreak. She had held it as long as she could – long enough to make a call – because there is only one thing worse than grieving – grieving alone.

Her grief was so intense that she could not speak – and all I could do was listen – and grieve with her – and dread. The list of potential explanations was not comforting – disease, drugs, pregnancy, failing grades, dismissal from school, death or injury to someone close to us. The sobbing subsided, temporarily, and the story began to come out. Haltingly, she told me that she had broken up with her boyfriend – not **just** a boyfriend, but a boy she had given her heart to, and hoped to marry – a boy she loved. She was devastated – I was relieved.

Thank God, I thought –
It's only that.

As she vented her frustration – because she didn't understand, her anger – because she felt betrayed, her loneliness and isolation – because it was her first time, and she thought she was the only one – as she talked – I realized what **distance** means – we were so far apart – and how little, practically, that I could do.

Can I come home? she said, *Dad, I just want to be in my own room and sleep in my own bed.*

Please - let me come home.

Oh, my dearest child, I thought, how I know what you're feeling – how I understand how a broken heart turns toward **home** - what a compliment to your mother and I that at the hour of your greatest need – you have remembered home, and turned to us. You need healing – and the balm of home is the only healing you know. But, my dearest, the world will not go away, and not even home can provide the medication you need.

Of course, I said, *Mom and I would love to see you.*

But even as I said it, my mind was leaping from the present to the future. I was aware of how much I **wanted** her to come home – how badly I **wanted** to provide the answers – to sooth and smooth and approve her. I **wanted** her to depend on **me** – to find her center in us – and even then, I knew that what **I** wanted – needed – was not what **she** needed. I knew that if she came home now – she would come home again – and again.

What would you do here, honey? You have no friends here – nothing to occupy your time – mom and I would have to work – what would you do all day?

I don't know, Dad, I just don't know what to do.

*I don't know either, but it seems to me that you would be very lonesome – and eventually, you'll have to go back. Wouldn't it be easier to face it now? You know, you **will** have to go back – don't you?*

I hadn't thought about that, she said, as though it was just now occurring to her that **her** world was the only one that had crashed and that even a crashed world would not prevent tomorrow. We talked on and on – and even as we talked – she grew up a little. New realities were making lasting impressions.

I guess there's no more coming home for me. Is there, Dad?

It was an aching question
and I ached in reply,
but I was glad that
she had asked it.

No, Kris, there's no more coming home.

Oh, my love, my baby, my darling girl – all things are struck real for you in this moment – it is a cruel world after all – now I was crying. Now we both know that you are beyond my healing – that even home, familiar walls, your own bed, and our love, are not enough to replace the emptiness that is in your heart. We were overwhelmed by our helplessness and our dependence.

Dad, will you and Mom pray for me?

We always do.

But, would you especially pray for me right now. It's the only hope I have.

Yes, it is the only hope we have ever had, but it takes times like these to realize it. You will forget - but the next time your heart breaks, you will remember more easily and you will turn in that direction more completely - and some day - when Mom and I are gone - that will truly be your only hope and refuge.

I'll be all right now, Dad. Don't worry.

Yes, I thought, *you'll be all right - not as you mean it, but you will be all right. Of course, that won't keep us from worrying - it's never that easy.*

I love you, Dad - more than ever.

I love you too. It was not the same thing - her love and mine - but it was closer than it had ever been - much closer. I hadn't moved much - but she had made a quantum leap.

I hung up and my wife - who was wide awake - said, *Is she all right? It's tough - hearing half a conversation. Yes, honey, she's all right - in fact, she's more all right than she's been in some time, but the next few weeks are going to be tough.*

Is she coming home?

No, she's not coming home - we've lost our baby - she's becoming - what we raised her to be - she's alright.

I wouldn't want to do it again - raise my kids I mean, but doing it has created a wonder - an understanding and a sense of dependence on God that I would never have had without it.

I'm Eighteen and Aching
Paul Simon, Art Garfunkel

IT'S A GOOD SONG - LIKE MOST Simon and Garfunkel - you have to be in the right mood, and you have to listen to the words. I hadn't heard it in a long time - years and years. I was traveling - alone. I had gone back to Michigan - to my birthplace - to my old houses and neighborhoods - to my old schools and church buildings. I walked the hallways, sat in my old desks, stood in the pulpits, went to the locker rooms, walked across the fields. I was home again. All of the old names and faces slowly returned. The giddy, exhilarating, unreasonable happiness, the sheer joy, power and strength of youth – falling in love and being invincible – I tingled with it. And the pain, the rejection, the losses, loneliness and bewilderment –

that came back too.

I went back on purpose. I wanted to find something that I had lost along the way – something I remembered but couldn't quite place or give a name to. It came to me at Wing Lake School on Fifteen Mile road – why there? – I don't know. I was only there part of one school year – my sixth grade year.

But it came to me there.

The old section of the school – where I attended – with the stone walls, and the huge windows and the bell tower is no longer used. But some thoughtful folks have preserved it. They gave me a key to my old classroom and I went in reverently. I found my old desk and I sat down. I remembered my teacher, my good friend Floyd Eslinger, and the athletic contests. As I sat there alone, in the dead silence, I remembered Kitty Proctor – my first love. Sitting there thinking about that time and remembering blond haired, blue eyed Kitty Proctor – it came to me. You see, Kitty Proctor was not only my first serious and romantic love – she was the last. I mean the last girl that I loved purely – innocently – before eros distorted my relationship with girls – and many other things as well. It was before I became selfish and manipulative in my girl relationships.

I went to the blackboard and I wrote my name and the date and left this message.

I loved Kitty Proctor here
without her ever knowing it.
I loved her purely, nobly,
innocently.
What I would give
to have that feeling
again.

Later, driving between Royal Oak and Rochester, I was listening to a tape and it was Simon and Garfunkel and *America*. A song about two graduated high schoolers who go to look for America. They hitchhike and take buses. I remembered doing that too – I hitchhiked from Royal Oak to Los Angeles. But it wasn't America

113

that I was looking for, and its really not America that these two are after. The most poignant words are;

Cathy, I'm lost, I said,
though I knew she was sleeping.
I'm eighteen and aching
and I don't know why.

I remembered being eighteen and aching and not knowing why - and now, I'm very much older and I still ache - in fact it's sometimes worse -

but now I know why.

I want to be innocent again -
I want to be free -
From my knowledge of evil,
From the experience of sin,
I want to be innocent again.

Thoreau was right, most men do lead lives of quiet desperation, swimming upstream against a relentless current, seeking a harbor of safety from that which overwhelms. It is innocence which motivates - impels us - driving us constantly on. We want to have peace, and peace is found in purity. That is why David cries;
Create in me a clean heart oh God,
And that is why Jesus says;
Blessed are the pure in heart, for they shall see God.
And that is why the apostle Paul says;
To the pure - all things are pure
to those who are corrupt -
there is nothing pure.
You never stop being a parent and now I know why. It's because you never stop learning and yearning - because sin and sorrow, desire, joy and regret come fresh upon us at many stages of life. Effective parents are constantly sharing their journey - even as I am sharing mine - with their children. They acknowledge that they are fellow pilgrims and in so doing they earn their children's trust and respect.

Aging

NO STEP ON THE ROAD TO accountability is more vital than the one introduced in this next story. The greatest deception of youth is that which tends to deny personal aging. A child has little comprehension of *getting older* in others and absolutely none in relationship to himself.

Without that first dawning of the relevance of passing time, accountability would never truly come into focus or take on practical meaning. We would always be able to postpone our day of reckoning and procrastinate with responsibility. The aging process, and its inevitable conclusion, dictates the parameters of our opportunities to live meaningful lives.

Every parent has many opportunities to impress this vital lesson on their children, without being morbid. The sickness or death of grandparents or other close family members or friends is a providential time to talk soberly about the meaning and purpose of life. Because of the sobriety of those occasions a lasting impression can be made.

All the Trumpets Sounded
On the Other Side

AFTER DINNER THEY TOOK THE walk as they always had. He knew nearly every step. What he waited for eagerly, were the stories his grandfather might tell as things along the way brought back memories. When the boy was small, they had lived quite close to his grandparents and the Sunday afternoon walks over the farm were regular. Now he lived far away and he only came during vacations and occasionally on holidays.

This is where your grandmother and I built our first house, it burned in 1937. If you look carefully, you can still see the corner of the old foundation. Or, *See the opening there in the barn right under the eave? That's a hay mow. Your father fell out of there when he was just about your size and broke his arm.* (The stories were much longer, but we have no patience for long stories.) *Oh, now dad,* the boy's father interrupted, *he doesn't want to hear that story again, you've told it ten times.* But the boy's father was wrong, and he wasn't only wrong, he wasn't telling the truth. It was he who didn't want to hear the story, it stirred too many painful memories of a happy past, of a life that was so different from his present one that it didn't seem possible that both lives could be lived by the same person. The stories reminded him of the contrast between what he had set out to be – and what he had become, and the contrast was not something he was comfortable with.

The boy hadn't realized it, didn't realize it now, but a sense of the significance of his family and history had come through those walks and stories. Now he was fourteen and in his jumbled, confused time of physical and mental transformation, the farm and his grandfather were things to hang on to. Although he would not have said so, he loved his grandfather, and he loved the stories.

As they approached the windmill, where the steep ascent to the upper pasture began, his grandfather paused, his thin white hair matted down with perspiration and his normally clear, bluegray eyes a little misty. *You and your dad go on up,* he said to the boy, *I think I'll just rest here and wait.* That had never happened before and as they walked away a very profound thought began to gather in the boy's mind. It gathered momentum as he and his father silently climbed to the pasture. Finally, unable to go further without hearing his thought out loud, he said,

Grandpa's getting old, isn't he?

What a whole world of budding maturity lay behind those words.

Yes, grandpa's eighty-five this year. The father was not close to his son because he was very busy and he had no time to tell him stories. Because he didn't know him, he failed to hear what was behind the question.

Do you think he minds?

Yes, I guess he does, he can't do much anymore and he knows most of his life is behind him. He spoke quickly and with some inner bitterness as though he did not wish to pursue the topic, but the boy could not turn loose of his thought.

You'll get old, too, won't you dad?

Yes, I guess I've already started, and it's not much fun. Again, the bitterness.

I can't believe I'll ever get old, but there was doubt in his voice.

It's hard when you're as young as you are and life is in front of you, in fact, I guess that's what being young is all about - everything is in front of you. Why, I remember... he began enthusiastically, but his voice trailed away. The boy had turned in anticipation, but his father finally shrugged and said,

Oh, forget it.

Two hours later, they returned to the windmill and found the old man asleep, huddled in a corner out of the wind, where the spring sun would fall on him, a shrunken bundle of faded blue denim cloth and wrinkled flesh. His head lay at a precarious angle and saliva dripped from the corner of his mouth. His breathing was so shallow that the boy feared he had died, but when he touched his shoulder, the kindly, thoughtful blue eyes blinked in the sun and he smiled. As they began the walk back, the boy, still pursuing his thought, expressed his concern with age. *Getting old must be terrible, Grandpa. Dad says that the worst thing is having all the important stuff behind you.*

The old man paused and looked long at his son and then at his grandson."I think your father has forgotten that I have been preparing for this all my life," he said solemnly, and *crossing the great river in front of me is the most important challenge of all.*

What river, grandpa?

Ask your father.

He needs to remember.

Goodness will Prevail

I WANT TO ASSURE YOU PARENTS that in this process of losing innocence, God will send periodic reassurances - positive events - into our children's lives to encourage them, and us, in our search for balance, meaning and peace. Awareness of the loss of innocence is absolutely necessary to motivate us in our search for what was lost. But without the reassurance of goodness and the potential of light, despair would cause us to give up the search. And so, in the midst of gloom - unlooked for, unhoped for, light comes - and when it finally dawns on us -

we realize that it was there all the time.

A critical role played by parents here, is in pointing out and applying the positive and providential things that God is doing. Often, children's eyes - unaccustomed to God's ways - need the practiced vision of a parent to see how God's love works.

Some of the great moments of my life have resulted from a childhood faith in the absolute power of goodness. My mother read to me about David and Goliath, Jepthah and Gideon. My own early reading about the search for the Holy Grail - the exploits of King Arthur and the knights of the roundtable - the conversion of Ebenezer Scrooge and the salvation of Hansel and Gretel, further confirmed my childhood notions. I believed completely that-

goodness would always prevail.

As I grew older and colder, the harsh realities of an evil and corrupt world shattered my naivete. I was easily duped and my credulity was taken advantage of by my friends and my enemies. Gradually, I was forced to acknowledge the power of evil. I became cynical and fearful, but occasionally events would take place which tended to restore my original faith.

This is one such event.

Dragons and Princesses

How should we be able to forget those ancient myths that are at the beginning of all peoples, the myths about dragons that at the last moment turn into princesses; perhaps all the dragons of our lives are princesses who are only waiting to see us, once beautiful and brave. Perhaps everything terrible is in its deepest being, something helpless, that wants help from us.

Rainer Marie Rilke

ALEC REDMON LIVED ON Rochester Road about a half mile from me. I had to pass his house on my way to school and on my way home. He was a bully. He had been held back in school and he was older, taller and stronger than the rest of us. He had threatened me, shoved me around, knocked my books out of my hands, knocked my hat off – he had baited and provoked me in every conceivable way, taunting and heckling and knowing that I dared not challenge his vastly superior size and strength. I was terrified of him. What he did to me physically was absolutely nothing to the mental anguish – the anxiety produced by my imagination every morning and afternoon.

In order to avoid him, I went blocks out of my way, taking long detours and varying my route so he would never know exactly which way I had gone. But one afternoon I forgot about Alec. I was so preoccupied with whatever thought I was pursuing, that I did not take any of my detours. I was not even aware of my mistake until I was shaken from my reverie by the sound of Alec's voice calling my name.

I stopped dead in my tracks, my heart beating wildly, my mind racing, my mouth suddenly dry and a nauseating sickness in my stomach. He ran across the road – right up to me and I prepared for the worst. He said, *Hey, John, we got that big test in history tomorrow and you're pretty good in there - would you come over tonight and help me study?*

I was stunned, absolutely speechless – Alec, obviously thinking that I would refuse, began to apologize for all of his meanness – he paused, looking down and he said quietly, *I really need some help, if I fail that test, I'm going to be held back again.* I mumbled a positive response, he thanked me and–

I went home very thoughtfully.

My walk to the Redmon's house that night was one of the most daring and brave things I ever did. Many things in my later life, which might appear to require courage, pale into insignificance in comparison to what it took to keep going that night.

The Redmon's had their porch light on and Mrs. Redmon met me at the door. I had never thought of Alec Redmon having a mother - it seemed incongruous. She was a very nice lady and she thanked me over and over for coming to help Alec. The Redmon house was much larger than ours but it smelled about the same, you know, all houses and families have a smell - that's how dogs know their owners - it's just that you get so used to your own smell that you don't notice it, but you sure notice other people's smell because it's different. The Redmon's house smelled different, but not much and it wasn't a bad difference.

Alec and I went up to his room to study. I could tell you a lot about his room - but it's enough to say that it was pretty much like mine.

What I found out, studying with Alec, was that he couldn't read. I couldn't believe it - I mean reading was the easiest thing in the world and it was fun too - and Alec couldn't read - not even the simple stuff. As I read to him and explained what the words meant and tried to help him understand about the Civil War and how it affected our country, something happened - it was not a conscious thought, but somehow I think that even then, I knew I would never be afraid of Alec Redmon - or any Alec Redmon ever again.

I could add that Alec and I became friends - pretty good friends, and remained friends until I moved away.

I ask you to read again the words at the beginning of this essay. I only pause to add that the world is full of dragons - Alec Redmon's - we are confronted with them at every turn. It is the mission of every Christian to learn and to show how Jesus converts them into princesses, not just by changing them, but by opening our eyes and changing us.

I also need to say that my faith in goodness has been restored. Oh, it has been refined and expanded, but it is much the same now as it was when I was a child.

Goodness **will** prevail.

Make no mistake about it.

There is an absolute power in

Goodness.

How could we possibly be disciples of Jesus and not believe that.

Jesus said that the meek would inherit the earth. The triumph of goodness is assured by God Himself because He **is** good, and just as surely as God lives, so goodness lives.

Do not be afraid to align yourself with goodness.
The victories of evil are short-lived
And self-destructive.

Goodness **Will** Prevail

He is There

IT WAS THE LOW POINT OF my young life. I was in my early twenties. I had been preaching for five or six years. I was unmarried - not by choice but by providence. A combination of finding myself at odds with some traditional understandings of scripture - unable to harmonize the realities of life with the unreality of many church traditions - the oppressing reality of sin in my life, not overt sin, as much as the depth of evil that I was capable of conceiving - my inability to deal with it or find cleansing - and the loss of a relationship with the girl I had hoped to marry - left me terribly depressed, lonely and emotionally disturbed.

In an effort to regain my balance I left home - all that was familiar and hitchhiked to Los Angeles. I had no specific destination or plan in mind. Los Angeles was the furthest place I knew and most of the rides I got were headed in that general direction.

After much shifting around - sleeping on park benches - on beaches and in Salvation Army centers, I found myself employed as a clean-up man at a mobile home factory in Lomita, California. I took a room at the Lomita Hotel, a shabby, disreputable establishment - which was home to several longshoremen - because it was cheap, they would wait till I got paid for their rent, and it was close enough to my work for me to walk.

I was friendless and broke.

I sold two or three articles of clothing I had for food money, but it didn't last. I found myself with four days to go until pay day and no money. I did okay the first day, but it was hot at work and my job demanded maximum physical exertion. After the second day, I was weak and a little dizzy. The third day I was desperate. I borrowed a dollar from one of the longshoremen and that night I went to the owner-operated diner just down the street. I sat on a stool at the counter.

Even in those days, a dollar didn't buy much. I went over the menu meticulously, trying to get the most for my dollar. I ordered a *pork dinner* and when it came I tried to eat slowly - savoring each bite.

While I was eating, I began to think about my mother's cooking - and I thought about home - church potlucks, singings, my friends, and what I used to be. The full realization of my lostness, hopelessness, and sinfulness settled over me. I saw clearly how far I had fallen and what I had become. A blanket of black depression, regret and guilt settled over me such as I had never experienced. I rested my head on my arms, which were placed on the counter, and I wept.

I had scarcely noticed that a man had come in and occupied the stool next to me. I became aware of him, when he turned and tried to console me in an almost unintelligible way. He was obviously very drunk. He had ordered the largest steak dinner on the menu and it was served to him just as I raised my head. He looked at it - shoved it across the counter - stated emphatically that he didn't want it - paid for it and left.

The owner-cook must have sensed my desperate condition as I stared unbelievingly at the forsaken plate.

You want this buddy?

It was delicious.

In some ways, a small gesture - but to a lost and wandering child - seeking a place to stand - a reason to be - it was a ray of hope. It was a friendly hand on my shoulder, a reassuring voice calling my name out of the darkness.

John. Son, I'm still here. Don't lose heart. I'm watching, I'm concerned - I'll see you through this.

I want you to see that **only** because of the accumulation of a thousand previous providences was I prepared to see the hand of God, in what ordinarily I would have tossed off as circumstantial. And He wasn't through - in fact He was just getting me ready for the next step. When I got back to the hotel, filled with the wonder and light of what had just happened, there was a letter from my mother, waiting for me.

Read this letter, parents - consider the circumstances in which I received it - and never question the value of your role or the providence which guides you.

Dear Son! (Date your letters)   Friday 19, 1962

Well, we just received your
letter (wish you would date your)
letters so I would know just
when you wrote.

Hope you are feeling lots better
and working real hard. God has
said to "Be content with such
things as you have, for, He has
said, I will never leave you, nor
forsake you." What a consolation.
This aught to comfort you, Son,
I know God will take care of you.
and He will bless you according
to, His Will. Love Him and Trust Him
and believe in Him, He will see you
through all your trials. I Pray
for you, Son, every Morning when
I am driving to work. When I
am working. When I drive home

A Letter From Home

THE FOLLOWING LETTER FROM MY mother was waiting when I returned to the hotel after eating. It appears here as close to its original form as possible and practical. I have spelled the words as she spelled them, and I have highlighted in bold print what she had underlined. One page in her original hand is included as well. My mother had only an elementary school education.

The *Hoy,* that she refers to is my brother-in-law, who is also a preacher.

Birmingham, is Birmingham, Michigan, close to where I grew up. My parents were *charter members* there.

Susie Q's is a fish and chips restaurant on Woodward Avenue just north of Ten Mile Road in Royal Oak, Michigan.

Sister Clyde Utley was the wife of Brother L.C. Utley, to whom I am deeply indebted. He was the preacher for at least two of the churches I attended as a boy. He was the first person to get me up front to lead singing and to answer Bible questions. He was the most kind, patient, loving, soft-spoken preacher I ever knew.

Mary Crosslin was the wife of Earl Crosslin and they were dear friends of my family at the Rochester church of Christ in Rochester, Michigan where Michigan Christian College is now.

My mother says – concerning the Bible she had received – that it was a *King James of course.* This is because we had a long standing feud in our house about *versions.* Hoy and I had both switched to the American Standard, which my mother considered scandalous. She would never read anything but the King James, which she felt had been used by the apostle Paul on Mars Hill. Hoy and I referred to her Bible as the *King James "Vision ,"* which did not help to resolve the argument.

I tell you these things to help you to understand how each name made an impact on me by stirring my memories of that happy time. I also know that every sensitive reader will learn much about the type of person my mother was.

A LETTER FROM HOME

Friday, Jan. 19, 1962
(Son, always date your letters)

Dear Son,

Well, we just received your letter (wish you would date your letters so I would know just when you wrote.)

Hope you are feeling lots better and working real hard. God has said to, *Be content with such things as you have, for, He said, I will never leave you, nor forsake you.* What a consolation. This aught to comfort you, Son, I know God will take care of you and He will bless you according to, **His Will**. Love Him and trust Him and believe in Him. He will see you through all your trials. I pray for you, Son - every morning when I am driving to work - when I am working - when I drive home at night - when I go to bed - when I wake up in the morning. I **know God** is with you, and I trust in Him to take care of you. I'm too far away from you, but God is everywhere. He knows where you are, what you are, and every move you make, so I pray to Him for you. May you get well, and be again a minister of the Gospel.

I must go to work so will write more when I have time.

Well, my day's work is done and I'm back home. Boy, it's cold here and snowing again. I'd like to finish this letter pretty quick and go to bed and keep warm under three blankets. Say, how are your clothes? Do you need more? How do you get them clean?

I'm glad to hear you have started working. Although I do not care for you in that kind of invirement, but as long as God is with you, all things will work out o.k., I know. Try hard to make the best of it, honey, and try to get a preaching job again. This would please God, and me too. Can't you wear work gloves in what you are working at?

Now, you asked me to read James 5:13-18 and I have just read it. Elias must have been a righteous man because the 16th verse says *The effectual fervent prayer of a **righteous** man availeth much.* Now my question is how **righteous** are you? Examine yourself. You should know the answer. You did a lot of good for the Lord when you were going about preaching the Word, comforting the sick, converting the sinners, but now you have left your first love, you have **quit**

working for the Lord, and instead have fallen in love in a worldly manner. Falling in love with a girl you would want to marry is alright, son, but to forsake the Lord's work is a sin. No man putting his hands to the plow and looking back is fit for the kingdom of Heaven. God has given you a talent. You worked with it for a while, but now you have buried it. Do you expect God to give you what you ask for when you have forsaken His commandments to go, preach the Gospel? These are straight forward questions, Son, but I hope they will help you see the light.

I just finished reading Ps. 27:1-14. Yes, Son, **wait** on the Lord. Be of **good courage wait**, wait on **the Lord** and He will give you strength. Read Ps. 28:7, and apply it to yourself. Ps. 34;17, 18, 19 These verses should give you strength. The 16th verse tells us that if we are evil the Lord will turn His face from us. The 18th verse gives you hope that God will be with you. The 19th verse the **righteous** have afflictions and **many,** but the Lord is there to deliver him **out of them** all. So Son, **believe** that **the Lord** will do this (if you are righteous).

Oh! I must go to bed it's 10:30 p.m. See you tomorrow (Lord willing).

Good morning. It's 7:50 a.m. Dad has left for work and I am back on the davenport where I slept all night. We had pancakes and sausage for breakfast. The Birmingham Church is having a fellowship dinner tonight at the Y.M.C.A. building in Birmingham. I am to take chicken and dressing, sure wish you could come too. I'm a little bit afraid of you being in such a ruff place, Son, but I keep telling myself that God will take care of you never mind where you are.

Son, until this thing happened to you, you were such a **good** sound **preacher** of the **Gospel** and a **wonderful teacher** and **song leader**. God gave you **all** these talents so you could use them in **His** service. Don't you know and realize that if you would pick up where you left off, and continue working with these talents in **His service** God will be more apt to answer your fervent prayers to Him.

You know the Bible well. It's up to you as a child of God to **go out** and **preach it. God** is holding you responsible. The scriptures tell Christians to **reprove, rebuke,** and **exhort** with **all** long **suffering**, and doctrine, and this is what I am **trying** to do for you, Son. Please think on these things.

Hoy, gave me a new Bible last Sunday (a King James of course) and it's so very nice. I think this is the fourth or fifth one I've had since becoming a member of God's Family. I've got them all saved and put away.

Son, you **must believe** and trust God in **every one** of the scriptures. Why do you question some of the scriptures. You say, *I believe or am at least **trying** too.* Every scripture is given to us by **God** and without **faith** it's **impossible** to believe in him. Why, Son, I **believe every word** that **God** has **written** in the **scriptures**. Do you believe me? You have known the Holy Scriptures from your youth, up. When you **couldn't read** or **write** I taught them to you. If I didn't believe in them would I have taken my time to teach them to you? I wish I could shrink you up to where you would be about two years old so I could start all over again to bring you up, knowing what I know now. I know that could never be so I must try my very best to convince you of where you have done wrong and are still doing wrong by forsaking the Lord's work.

Sunday night, 7:30, Dad is in bed snoring away and I'm on the davenport again, all ready for bed, just wanted to finish this letter so I can get it mailed early in the morning.

We didn't go to church tonight, Dad had a very bad headache and the weather is sort of freezing rain. We had dinner with the Moody's after church today. Went to Susie Q's. Then we all went to a singing at Rochester. Mary Crosslin asked me to say *Hello* to you for her and that she is praying for you. Sister Clyde Utley said the same thing. Every where we go some one or more ask us how you are. There are so many of your brethren that are very much concerned about you. I tell them you are making out o.k., or something to that effect. I hope, I'm not wrong in telling them this much about you. I would love to tell all who ask me how very well you are doing and feeling real proud of such a wonderful son. I pray God that He will give you strength and help you through this terrible ordeal that has such a bearing on you, and keeping you so tied up in a knot.

Honey, I want you to try real hard to get along on your own. I have faith in you and all the confidence in the world that you can make it by yourself.

Well, Sweetie, I've enjoyed writing this letter to you although it's taken me three days off and on but I'm about to sign off.

I sent my first letter to Pepperdine, the second to the Hotel where you are staying. Hope you got them both. You know your Aunt Beulah is living in El Cerrito. Is this any where near you? Gee, but I wish I could see you. Seems like such a long time since you left home. We are thinking about putting our property up for sale soon as we can clear it up a bit. Dad is working good now during this real cold spell. Well, Son, please try to make it on your very own. All things will work out for **good** because I know you love the Lord.

Bye, write us soon.

Lots of love,
Mom and Dad

Do Your Children Know the Lord?

THE BIBLE CHARGES PARENTS with the responsibility of training, instructing and disciplining their children. 1 Samuel 2:12 says, *Now the sons of Eli were worthless men, they did not know the Lord.* The rest of that chapter is a sobering one for parents because Eli is charged by God with dereliction of duty. He is held directly and personally responsible for his son's behavior.

Do *your* children know the Lord?

Did you know *you* were responsible for that?

How do you teach children to know the Lord? The first prerequisite is, of course, to know Him yourself. Books and classes on parenting skills will never lead to sustained success until we absorb the big class on Godliness. You can't pass calculus until you succeed at arithmetic. God is the *great parent*. By knowing *Him* we learn the basics of good parenting. Every attempt to improve parenting skills, must begin with a study of God.

Most popular concepts of parenting have this glaring deficiency – they view parenting as an isolated activity – unrelated to the speech, habits and behavior of parents in their other roles. We view parenting like we view sports heroes, doctors and actors. We tend to believe that success in those areas makes people experts in every area – so if a prominent actor, athlete or politician endorses a product or philosophy – it gives it credibility. We fail to realize that a person may be a world class chess player, actor, surgeon, diplomat, or athlete and still be a world class jerk as a person.

That is not so with parenting.

Good parenting skills are not confined to parenting. They cannot be put on and taken off – like sports equipment, surgeon's gloves, political speeches and T. V. faces – as the occasion demands. They must be woven into the fabric of our personality. The glaring parental failures of Eli, Samuel, David and Solomon do not prove that the best of parents can have rotten kids - they do prove that even spiritually committed people can fail to be Godly parents.

The books published by sport's heroes do not create sport's heroes - unless you are first a great athlete. Child raising advice is about the same. Unless you are the right kind of person - the *tricks* of the trade aren't going to help much. Books, seminars and sermons have not stemmed the rising tide of parental failure because the folks who listen and read do not change their life styles. They want a quick fix - handy dandy formula - they want to *patch it, blow it up and drive it away.* The first thing you must decide is not - *do I want to be a better parent?* - but,

do I want to be a better person?

But, you say, does that mean that great parents - like great athletes - are born? No, praise God, the stuff that great parents are made from comes from being *born again* - a deliberate choice to incorporate divine standards into our lives.

I am often asked why the Bible doesn't give more *how to* answers to specific parenting questions. I believe that God knew how many variables there were in that process. Differences in personalities, environment and abilities make it impossible to hand down a, *what everybody always wanted to know about raising children, in five easy steps,* guidebook. That is precisely why the nice, neat formula's like *terrible twos, frustrating fours* and *fascinating fives,* make for good dialectics but absolutely awful parenting.

God has given us divine principles and the intellectual and emotional ability to understand them and put them into practice. Let me call your attention to three Biblical principles which will demonstrate my point. These principles are vital to good parenting - but they are also vital to the larger arena of successful living. They can be taught -

but they must first be **lived**.

Balance! Balance! Balance! The divine quality of equilibrium - of finding what is reasonable - in work, recreation, food, discipline, sex, music, clothes, education - in life. The Divine Nature is carefully balanced. God is the God of the *right amount.* Evidence of balance is found in every aspect of creation and we have found that when we unbalance either nature or our lives - we suffer. Good parenting is balanced - balanced between *yes* and *no*; balanced between what **you** decide and what **they** decide; balanced between their **wants** and their **needs**; balanced between what is good for

them and what is good for **others**; balanced between **vegetables** and **desert**: balanced between what is **acceptable** and what is **unacceptable**: balanced between **freedom** and **responsibility**.

The second divine principle is that of consistency or dependability. God's word is good – and the word of parents should be good – both *yes - no - perhaps -* and *if you do that, I'll whip you.* Inconsistency creates confusion and breeds frustration. Children want to know where the boundaries are, and once they learn them, they want them to stay put. God's promises are good and our confidence in Him rests on His total dependability. Parents who allow themselves to be talked into or out of promises – or act upon whims, create very tenuous and uncertain children. As parents – promise less – deliver more, do not be controlled by the emotion of the moment, but rather be controlled by the basic principles of who you are and what kind of family you are building.

The third principle is that of **responsibility**. Parents have become **producers**. They have produced children and then they have turned them over to the institutions to do the mothering and fathering. We rely on Day Care to potty train them and teach them to play fair. We rely on the public school system to teach them social skills – basic hygiene, geography, morals, historical perspective and educate them about sex. We rely on television to entertain them, challenge them, and give them values. And as parents, we provide a bed, clothes, spending money, food, a T.V., a VCR, and a car.
So when things go wrong –
We blame the institutions.

Remember, God holds parents directly responsible for their children.

Do *your* children know the Lord?

Who Is Responsible?

MY OLDEST SON WAS IN THE fourth grade. He attended the Maize Unified School District Elementary School, in Maize, Kansas. It was a town of about eight hundred souls I think, although some of them did not know that they had souls, or at least they *acted* as though they did not. But I suspect that it was about like most other towns in that respect. The town was named after the grain which occupied the labor, time, attention and conversation of nearly every resident, because their financial well-being and future expectations were tied directly to that product.

It was a good enough school, probably above average as schools go, but at some point I began to be troubled by certain of my son's comments and attitudes. Nothing outlandish, just a cumulative series of minor incidents which individually would be passed off as inconsequential. I decided to investigate by going to visit with his teacher, which I hoped would put my mind at rest.

I called the school and made an appointment to come the following day, but my apprehension was increased when the teacher returned my call that evening to ask why I was coming. I explained my concern in very non-threatening terms and assured him that I had no reason to doubt either his interest or his competency. He tried to assure me that all was well and that there was no reason for me to come. The more he talked, the more determined I was to go. We made an appointment for the next day right after school.

I intentionally arrived early and stood just outside the classroom door in the hallway. Through the window in the door, I had a clear view of nearly the whole classroom and since the students were seated with their backs to the door, I could watch and listen unobserved.

The classroom was a disaster, it looked like it had been vandalized, and I guess it had. Chairs and desks were in an incredible state of disarray. While the teacher talked, not a single student paid the slightest attention to him. They talked openly to each other, they turned their backs to him, walked around the room, laughed loudly, threw paperwads, and while he read from the textbook, not one student even had theirs open. My son was an integral part of the chaos.

When the dismissal bell rang, they stampeded into the hallway, milling, shouting and shoving like corralled cattle. Fortunately for me, I am rather large and probably somewhat intimidating to a fourth grader, so they parted around me like an avalanche around a ponderosa pine. The fact that I collared the first little scoundrel that stepped on my freshly shined boots and threatened to thrash him soundly, probably had a sobering effect on the rest of them.

My son, who had no idea that I was coming, stopped short when he saw me, and the – "caught in the act," look on his face, further convinced me that I had done the right thing. I told him to wait in the hall until I was through and we would ride home together.

I introduced myself to the teacher. He was still sitting behind his desk, with a look of mixed apology, bewilderment and relief on his face – he had survived another day. I again expressed my concern about my son. He said that my son was doing pretty well academically, especially compared to the others, and he produced his gradebook to prove it. He said that my son's behavior was no worse than most and better than many and that all in all I had nothing to worry about.

When I expressed my horror at what I had witnessed through the window, he explained in some detail that this particular class of fourth graders had been hellions since kindergarten and that no one had ever been able to do anything with them, he had quit trying. He told me that I had simply been unfortunate to have a fourth grader instead of a third or fifth. I listened as patiently as possible, but finally I said,

> Mr._____, you need to understand one thing. I am concerned with only one student in your class, and in this school for that matter, and that is *my son*. His behavior and his achievements are not to be measured by any standards other than those of his family, his religion, and his personal capabilities. My son's behavior in your class is reprehensible, his lack of respect for your position is intolerable, his academic achievement is shameful, and I hold you personally responsible for allowing this situation to develop, for tolerating it, and for not informing me about it. You will see an immediate change in my son's behavior and attitude – that is **my responsibility**. I will expect a regular report from you about his progress in these other areas – that, and the behavior and respect of the rest of these students is **your responsibility**.

This teacher had abdicated. He had signed a contract, given his word and accepted pay to be a teacher, with all the inherent duties and obligations that that implies, and now when things were tough, he refused to accept responsibility for his failures and blamed the outcome on former teachers, parents and his students.

I get so discouraged with parents who blame all of their problems on public education, society, the church, the environment, the government, or some new medical analysis. When people elect to have children, they make a *covenant* which obligates them to a position of total *personal responsibility* for those children - for every aspect of what it means to grow from infancy to maturity - for their morals, their manners, their attitudes, their academic achievement, their intellectual and imaginative stimulation, and for their spiritual foundations. Listen to God's instructions to the parents of Israel;

> These words I command you today,
> shall be in your heart;
> You shall teach them diligently
> to your children.
> You shall teach them diligently
> to your children.

Imagination

IMAGINATION - ONE OF GOD'S great gifts - a gift which separates us from all other created things - a gift without which there would be no dreams, no maybes, no tomorrow, no invention, no literature, no cure, no need, no promise, no reason, no might have been, no salvation, no nobility, no rising above. It would be a frightfully dull world without imagination - a type of hell, where every day would be lived with the same mathematical predictability, that dominated the previous one.

Every child has an imagination. My word to you parents is to feed and foster it - let it sprout wings and lead your child into worlds that no one else has ever discovered. Imagination is the final frontier - an ever expanding westward movement that will not end abruptly, frustrated by a Pacific Ocean. Never forget that the basic christian attributes of faith, hope, and love are all tied irretrievably to imagination.

God himself, is seen through the imagination, since it is impossible to conceive Him through sight and touch. There are so many biblical illustrations - but let me use only one. Acts seven contains Stephen's sermon and it ultimately records his murder. As the Jews stone him to death, he points toward the sky and says, *Look, I see the heavens opened and Jesus standing at God's right hand*. But when those who were stoning him looked in the direction he was pointing - they saw nothing! I want to ask you why? Was it a trick of the eyes? If the heavens were really open and Jesus was standing by God's throne and Stephen could really see it - why couldn't the Jews?

Was it because their lifeless legalism
Did not permit any imaginative flights?

I do not speak of a world of make-believe, what Stephen saw was a far greater reality than the surrealistic, transitory, and shadowy things which constantly keep us focused on the mundane. When Jesus told His disciples to look at the birds, or to look at the fields - what was He calling them to do? They had seen thousands of birds and many fields. What did Jesus mean when he said of the Jews that they had eyes which saw but did not perceive?

I tell you parents, the fact that they could not or would not see, kept them from the Kingdom of God. I tell you also that the seeing that Jesus refers to is tied to imagination - the gift God gave us so that we could understand all of His other gifts. The gift which creates endless possibilities and which leads us to the throne of God.

Encourage your child's imagination - if you ridicule it and hinder it - if you cover it up with, "hard realities," you shouldn't wonder that the church, faith, salvation and hope don't seem to have much meaning in their lives.

I'm Sorry They Told Me

*When **I consider** your heavens,*
  the work of your fingers,
The moon and stars,
  which you have set in place,
What is man that you are mindful
  of him?

Ps. 8:3,4

EVERY SPRING I LOOKED FOR THE robins. It was sort of a big thing in my family as to who would see one first. One evening at the supper table, one of us would announce - rather proudly, *I saw a robin today,* and we would talk excitedly about spring. Sometimes they would come when there were still patches of snow around, but spring could not be far.

Late that fall, they would disappear, not all at once - they would just be fewer and fewer, then one day you would realize that they were gone. When I asked about where they went, my mom said, *South.* The only south I knew about was Maynard, Arkansas and I had visions of my uncle Clarence's farm being inundated with millions of robins. How did they find it? Were there bird roads with atlases? How did they know it was time to go, or to come back? Were the robins I saw this year the same ones as last year – or new ones? My mom didn't know and I was filled with **wonder** at such a mystery.

When I got older, they told me. I learned all the answers – the places they went and why. The mystery was solved and I didn't **wonder** anymore, so the robins didn't mean so much and the coming of spring lost some of its glory.

I'm sorry they told me.

I went through the same process with the Canadian Geese. They didn't live around our house, but they passed, high above, calling continuously to each other, *This way - this way, Not much further, Almost there - follow Jack up there, he knows the way.* When it was clear and the moon was bright, I could see them out of my bedroom window always in their semi *V* formation, with one end of the *V* always longer than the other. I wondered if they had lost somebody – if some old warrior had dropped out and said, *You'll just have to go on without me, this year,* and his side of the line had tightened up a little, leaving space at one end, so that if he caught up he would know that they wanted him. I loved the geese, and yearned to fly with them. I **wondered** about where they went – and why.

They told me about the geese too – I didn't **wonder** anymore about them – I lost my urge to fly – but I still loved them. They couldn't take that away from me.

I'm sorry they told me.

People were always explaining things to me. Oh, they meant well, and there is much that needs explanation. Sometimes though, I think it would have been better if they had let me **wonder** – if they had said, *Don't look too far, or too deep, leave it there and **wonder** about it.* It is **wonder** that brings us close to God. Enjoy the **wonder** of it. You are not better for knowing, and knowledge is very deceptive, and often empty.

Now, I come to *faith* and the *New birth*, and *resurrection*. The shelves of bookstores are filled with *What Is* books. Lots of folks trying to do with these ideas what they did to me with the robins and the geese. But they can't you know. They're trying to write *How To* manuals for the mysteries of knowing God.

It won't work this time. They really didn't know as much about the robins and the geese as they let on – and now they're really over their heads. Please, don't let any drug store, textbook, theological technician, take the **wonder** and the excitement out of your personal walk with God. Don't let them explain prayer, heaven, providence and sonship to you to the extent that you are no longer excited by the endless possibilities that the concept of, "knowing God," should arouse in you.

> **Consider** *the lilies of the field,*
> *how they grow.*
> *They toil not, neither do they spin,*
> *And yet I say, unto you*
> *That even Solomon in all his glory*
> *was not arrayed like one of these.*
> Matt. 6:28-29

Teach your children to *consider,* to *wonder* and to *imagine.* Teach them that God is a God of **wonder** - that they will never *know the Lord* until they have learned the power of **possibility**.

Where Did It Go?

SHE HAD TAKEN THE BOY to the holiday pageant because she wanted to be a good mother. It was about what she expected - poorly done, old costumes, missed lines, a hackneyed, trite repeat of familiar words and tunes. The boy had been fascinated by the star. It was the only really well done piece in the set. Someone had obviously put some time and thought into it. It revolved, sparkling and twinkling, constantly bringing back even an unwilling gaze. The boy had asked about it and she had given the old stock answer.

She was relieved when it was finally over.

It was dark when they left, very dark, and very cold, but it was marvelously clear. She hurried toward the car and regretted that she had had to park so far away. She kept his hand in hers and when he stumbled she almost fell with him. *Watch where you're going,* she said, perhaps more crossly than she had intended. She stopped to help him to his feet.

I was looking for the star, he said apologetically

Why there's millions of them, she misunderstood.

I was looking for His star, he corrected.

Oh, don't be silly, that was just a play, people acting, the star went away long ago.

Where did it go? He was disappointed, but continued to look.

I don't know, honey, it just went away. Come on now, we've got to hurry.

Maybe it's that one, he pointed to a particularly bright, friendly star. *Is that Jesus' star?*

No, it's not Jesus' star. It's just a star.

But it could be His star, he insisted. *Maybe it's come back.*

Across her consciousness there flashed a thought. Where it came from, who could guess? Some might say that the Spirit, ever watchful, never sleeping, seized this precious moment when her guard was down and kindled into flame a thought, a thought which had lain dormant for years.

Oh God, she thought, *I wish it was His star, I wish it had come back, I wish I could believe in it like I used to.* She did not say it, but it was there – and then it was blotted out by cold, fatigue, and pressing cares – but not completely. It was a prayer, and it was heard in the heart of Him who hears and understands. Before she had thought of what to say to her son, His messengers were speeding faster than light to respond.

At the boy's insistence, she finally looked up, and there *was* a star! I mean, it was as different as a bonfire is from a kitchen match. She glanced quickly down at her small son, and the soft iridescent glow of the star seemed to cast a gentle halo of light all around him. And then it was gone and she shook her head like one who wishes to make certain of their alertness.

When they got home, she was still troubled by it. She helped the boy to undress and she tucked him in with more care and tenderness than usual. When he asked her to help him with his prayers she did – and she added a special new prayer of her own.

Dear Father, she said, *thank you for tonight.*

When she returned to the living room her husband said, *Well, how did it go?*

Oh, about the same as last year - except, her voice trailed off into silence and she couldn't find a way of finishing. He looked up from the show he was watching.

Except what? Did something happen?

No, not really - well, she paused, her heart beating wildly because she knew she was leaping into the darkness - she picked up the remote control and flipped the T.V. off.

Yes, she said, *something **did** happen, Andy - at least I think it did - but that really doesn't matter, what matters is that we need to talk.*

And they did, you know.

At some point in every holiday season, I find myself gazing at the stars. They seem especially close and significant when it's cold and silent. I think I want to see *that* star, at least to imagine the **wonder** of it, as it makes its majestic and purposeful way to its appointed destination. There, where it concentrates its glorious radiance on the holy ground, is where Jesus was born. God, calling to us –

Look over here,

See my Incarnation.

It's not too hard for me to believe in *that* star. My child's heart, awakened from months of slumber by this blessed season, is fully confident that its guiding light brought those *wise men* to worship Jesus. I wonder though, where did it go? Does He still move stars to His purpose? Is there yet a light calling us to Bethlehem? Does His star, which winks and beckons, not shine for us because we have grown so mature and practical that we dismiss it, as Scrooge dismissed his ghosts, by uttering a *humbug* of disbelief?

The star was for **all** to see, but only the *wise men* were guided by it. When they arrived, they did not find countless multitudes of other seekers who had followed its light. Has our wisdom failed us? Perhaps the beckoning, guiding light of God's special star is there yet, but our eyes are not pointed upward to Him, - because we do not believe in stars. Our eyes look inward to our own wisdom, and outward to our own light, and around us to the light and wisdom of men like ourselves. And all the while, God calls us by His light, pleading with us to look upward to His holiness.

A child's imagination is a marvelous gift of God. Encourage it, strengthen it. The world will be struck real all too soon, you needn't worry about that. Much of our relationship with God falls into the realm of what Paul calls a *mystery*, and many never enter the Kingdom because it is nonsense, to their practical, factual mind sets.

Sometimes we would all do well to see God through the eyes of a child. Alltogether too many imaginations are ridiculed and discouraged by parents who no longer have the capacity to dream.

Where Did It Go?

Flags Do Not Win Wars

HOLIDAYS, LIKE THE FOURTH of July, are not without opportunity to teach important lessons that leave lasting impressions. During this holiday, flags will be displayed everywhere and children's curiosity will be aroused. Children wonder about symbols – whether they ask about them or not. Explaining about the flag, how and who conceived it, and what it stands for can lead to a better understanding of Christian symbolism – its meaning and purpose.

When I was in the sixth grade, I attended Northwood Elementary School. It was on Twelve Mile Road in Royal Oak, Michigan. At some point, in an otherwise lackluster career, I received the high distinction of being appointed as a safety patrol. It was a much coveted position of admiration and power as well. I was exceedingly proud of my AAA belt and the red flag I used to stop traffic. The power to stop traffic was particularly gratifying and I fear it made me somewhat arrogant. Power corrupts! I even stopped traffic when I didn't need to, and held it longer than necessary, just to prove that I could. Adults might fume, blow their horns, or even shout, but they were very intimidated by a sixth grade safety patrol.

Another part of being a patrol boy was the responsibility of putting up the flag, taking it down, and carefully folding it for the next day's use. I remember our principal, Mr. Dykstra, calling us in and reviewing the flag procedures. He was a tall, slender, austere man who was from the old school. Consequently, he was more interested in our *respect* than our *companionship,* and in being *principal* than being a *pal*. He was very serious, and when he laid his hand on the folded flag, it was like he was touching a Bible or some great family treasure, and I guess he was. He gave us a little speech about the flag – about how important it was – and what it stood for. He told us he had served in World War II – that his brother had been killed in the Philippines and that he had the flag that the government had draped over his brother's coffin. He told us to never – never – ever allow the flag to touch the ground –

and we never did.

We would get to school thirty minutes early to get the flag, unfold it, hook it to the rope, then – slowly – we would raise it – watching it gradually unfurl, catch the wind, and begin its gentle, undulating motion. It was a grand thing, to see it there, high above us, with the morning sun glistening on the white stars and stripes. I would get all tingly - and goose bumpy, nearly every time.

I have always revered the flag, and I wonder why? I mean, after all, its just a symbol, and flags do not win wars. When, during the seventies, I began to see flags sewn on the seat of people's jeans, it bothered me - I didn't like it. And when I read of flag burnings it made me sad - and mad, because to me the flag stands for good things - what is best about us. It is a symbol-

but the things it stands for are real.

We need to be careful with our symbols - we must not take them lightly. We err when we think that symbols have no substance - that icons have no real power. Ideas - emotions are real things, and the symbols which represent them are so closely tied to the things themselves, that we cannot destroy the symbols, without doing irreparable damage to the ideas.

Those of us who are Christians should know it better than anyone. We have two great symbols - the Lord's Supper and baptism. Even though they have no substance in themselves - there is no salvation in crackers, grape juice, or water - they are no less real. When I think of assembling with God's family, and someone saying:

> *Today, we're just going to think about the crucifixion, for five minutes - we're going to eliminate all that unnecessary, empty symbolism. Grape juice and matzos cost money, not to mention the hassle of preparation, clean up, and the loss of time in passing it out - we can do just as well by simply thinking about it.*

But we can't!

Jesus said, *Do this in my memory,* and it is well that we do. He said, *This is my body and my blood,* and although we understand the symbolic part, we also understand that because we call it a *symbol,* it is no less real to those who see in it the cross, the blood, the empty tomb, the church, forgiveness and hope.

What I'm saying is, that while it is true that we must not worship the symbols, because that is idolatry, we must not fail to take them seriously, because that is foolishness. We need the symbols - they are absolutely critical to us. Without them, we would soon forget who we are, and even-

why we are.

I think that one of the hardest things I had to confront, in my spiritual, and physical immaturity, was Christian symbolism. Things like the flag, the eagle, and the statue of liberty, present wonderful opportunities for parents to draw parallel lessons to enhance their children's understanding.

I wonder, do flags win wars?

Halloween

PERHAPS, LIKE ME, YOU DON'T know exactly what to do with Halloween. I'm fortunate in that my children are all grown and I have no grandchildren - yet, so the event sort of just passes me by - but not quite,
> it's never that simple.
When I was a kid, I was blissfully ignorant of the sinister implications of this holiday. I didn't know the origin of Halloween and wouldn't have cared if I had. Narrow faced, long, warty nosed, toothless witches with tall, pointed hats, astride broomsticks or hovering over boiling cauldrons of magical potions - muttering,
> *hubble, bubble, stubble,*
> *cat's brew and witches stew,*
or some other secret incantation - were part of that beautiful mythology which contained Paul Bunyan, Johnny Appleseed, Robin Hood, the Lone Ranger and a host of other fictional characters which soon enough would take their places on the dusty shelves in the attic of my memory. Shelves which already held Puff - the magic dragon, Jolly Old Saint Nick and the Tooth Fairy.
> It was part of growing up.
I am saddened that the world has grown older and colder and infinitely poorer, because of a need for cynical adults to debunk every potential flight of a child's imagination, leaving them only the cold, sterile, antiseptic, but stark realities of the adult world. Everything must be analyzed, dissected, and labelled.
> Being a child,
> is not near
> so much fun,
> as it used to be.
So now the adults have taken over Halloween. It is no longer a

simple - innocent meandering through a mythological forest of Jack-O-Lanterns - candied apples - cider and doughnuts - putting on your mother's make-up, and your dad's old clothes - laugher, trick or treating, pranks, and a chance for the neighbors to treat the local children and pretend they don't recognize them.

Commercial interests saw that big bucks could be made by exploiting the basic ingredients of the holiday. They began hawking their wares in an unconscionable way, persuading gullible and all too willing parents that **their** candy, pumpkins, costumes and paraphernalia were much easier - if not cheaper - and infinitely more desirable and impressive in their detail, than the home made stuff, which had been so much a part of what made the holiday special for earlier generations.

The movie industry wasn't far behind big business. They saw the possibility of capitalizing on the bizarre, macabre aspects of Halloween and produced movies which exaggerated the mysterious, other worldly overtones - perverting simple, even innocent concepts, and converting them into mass hysteria. Witches, warlocks, goblins, and ghastly deeds - were made so frighteningly real and possible that the mythological aura which had previously existed was destroyed. Again - blissfully ignorant parents delivered their sacrificial lambs to the theater's or to the T.V. to have their children's worst nightmares made into a visual reality.

Of course religion got involved. Even well-meaning religionists felt it necessary to tell how the holiday began and to explain all of the sinister implications of that auspicious beginning. Anti-religionists threw historical facts about the theological implications of Halloween at religionists so that they could prove their inconsistency, and some thoroughly evil people started taking the ancient, superstitious traditions seriously, developing rituals to really worship and appease the prince of demons.

Well, it's all screwed up - there's no doubt about that. What to do? There is no nice, neat, all-inclusive, all purpose answer. Halloween won't go away - I wish it would - and you can't ignore it - anymore than you can ignore the Super Bowl or the World Series, and there are some similarities between Halloween and the Super Bowl.

I think what we can do is try to remain pure. *To the pure, **all things** are pure - but to him who is **defiled** - there is **nothing** pure.*

Specifically, my advice is; let the children enjoy the wholesome aspects of this holiday and don't mar their innocence with all of the sinister implications, they will grow old and cynical soon enough.

Those children who are old enough to be leaving things like Halloween behind, should be given straight answers and relevant information which will dispel mistaken notions they may have retained.

Personally, I wish I could return to a simpler world, but I cannot. We have lost our innocence and we must make our way without it as best we can-

until He calls us home.

CHAPTER
8

A Sense of Humor

THERE ARE FEW PARENTING TOOLS that equal the value of a sense of humor. Few things in life can take the tension from the atmosphere – change disaster into victory – restore wounded pride – relieve the burden of guilt and bring people into closer union – than genuine, good natured laughter.

The ability to see what is humorous is a gift of God. Human beings are ridiculous, and if we could only let our pride down for a moment and have a good laugh at ourselves we could heal more woes with it than a thousand psychoanalysts.

These next stories are simply indicative of the types of situations – most of them **very** serious at the time – which viewed from a more distant perspective are truly funny and deserve laughter much more than chagrin. May God help us – even at the moment – to laugh and to teach our children the value of laughter – to laugh at themselves and to enjoy the instant release which laughter brings.

Jary and the Belt – Good Times

MY SISTER, JARY, IS THE best person I ever knew, and she has had a remarkable effect on my life for good. I never knew her to do anything wrong or even to think a wrong thought, which put considerable pressure on me, because I did much of both. Anyway, she is a remarkable person. I don't mean that I thought that way when I was a kid, or that it was always sweetness and light between us, or even that I loved her for her gracious attempts to help me with my manners, my dress, my speech, my homework, my friends, my

conduct in church, at school and every place else, brushing my teeth, taking more baths, combing my hair, cleaning my room - and every other area of my personal conduct.

Now there you go - I know what you're thinking - you're thinking I was a slob, a recalcitrant deadbeat. Well, you're dead wrong, I wasn't nearly that bad - it's only that some folks have got more refined notions of propriety than others - you take my belt for instance.

Be patient, I'll try to make this worth your while.

I had this great belt, got it from my Uncle Art who was an alcoholic. Originally it was about twenty-two and one half inches too long for my girth (that's the distance around your waist), but it never bothered me in the least. I was proud of that belt. It was handier than a whistle on a plow. When I was bored, or trying to impress the girls, I would just unlimber that extra twenty-one inches and I would twirl it, while I whistled *Yankee Doodle*. (I know you're wondering what happened to the other inch and a half. You'll have to wait till the next story.) I thought that twirling that belt was just about the neatest thing ever imagined, and many of the girls my age thought so too. Why Becky Swarthout told me one time that it just gave her the cold shivers to watch me. What I want to get at is, that my sister just about had a coronary every time. She was **mortified, embarrassed, humiliated**. *Look there, Mom, he's doing it again.* And, of course, my mother always saw her side of it.

To shorten this story, let me tell you that they plotted against me. One day I was standing as nonchalantly as you can imagine, leaning against the door-jam in the kitchen, twirling my belt and whistling *Yankee Doodle* for all I was worth. There wasn't anybody to impress. I was doing it because of the sheer joy I got out of it, and it's possible that I may have been trying to aggravate, just a tad. My very own mother sidles up to me and suddenly grabs me and pins my arms, my sister sneaks up behind and trips me up, I am wrestled to the floor, and as I lay screaming bloody murder, they cut my belt off with a butcher knife.

I believe a psychologist could have a picnic with this tale and could explain much of my unusual behavior in later life, due to this emotional trauma inflicted upon me in my formative years. It was like a death. I mourned the loss of my belt for at least thirty-two years. I kept the piece they cut off - for nearly a week, and then discovered that it made an excellent pocket for a slingshot I was making.

Trimming Spot's Tail

I'M SURE YOU'VE BEEN WAITING with breathless anticipation to find out what happened to the other inch and a half of my belt. Well, I lost that inch and a half in an accident. You see, we had this dog named Spot - he was solid black. Why did we call him Spot? - because he looked like one - that's why. He had an unusually long, heavy, shaggy, black tail. It was out of proportion to his body. Spot's tail was troublesome. He wagged it constantly and it knocked stuff off of tables, it got long black hair on your trousers and the furniture-
and it looked weird.

My dad finally decided that Spot would be much better off - and so would we - if he cut off about half of his tail. He decided to wrap my belt around Spot's tail to keep it from bleeding too much, and to sort of serve as a marker for where he wanted to cut it off.

I was a little worried about Spot because it seemed to me that a tail amputation might be pretty unsettling - painful even. My father assured me though - that dogs didn't have much feeling in their tails-
I felt a lot better.

It was quite an event, all of my boyfriends came over - I could have sold tickets - if I'd been thinking. We laid old Spot down and stretched out his tail on a two by four - it looked like a big black sausage - with hair. I told Spot what my dad had told me about dogs not having any feeling in their tails, but it didn't seem to help him like it had me. Spot just laid there, sort of quivering -
he knew something was up.

My father was determined to do his work with one whack, so he raised the axe high above his head and took careful aim. I think that right at that moment, he might have wavered a little in his resolution, because he paused when the axe reached its highest point - but with all of us standing there, he sort of had to see it through. I was stroking Spot's head and talking to him - reassuring him that this would only take a minute and wouldn't hurt at all and besides we'd all be happier afterward. But out of the corner of his eye he saw my dad - standing over him with that axe raised in a threatening position. From Spot's vantage point it may not have been exactly clear what my father was aiming at. As the axe descended, Old Spot yelped like he'd been stung by the Great White Hornet - and he jumped. My dad almost missed - but not quite. He cut off seven inches of Spot's tail and an inch and a half of my belt.

In spite of my father's assurance that dogs have no feelings in their tails, Spot sure did take on. It may have just been an act – to gain sympathy – but he shot around the yard, yelping and howling like all the demons in hell were after him. I never saw a dog take on so. He even tried to bite where his tail used to be – which was hilarious to us –

but Spot didn't seem to think so.

Now you would think that he would have been grateful for the attention that we showered upon him, plus the fact that he had been made more agreeable to us at very little expense to him – he wasn't. That fool dog became very suspicious of us. I never did understand it. He wouldn't allow my father to come within ten feet of him as long as he lived, and every time we picked up the axe he left the yard fairly humming, and didn't come back for three days. I think he even resented me, for laughing at his antics–

which was totally unreasonable.

You know, we're always willing to make changes in other folks so as to make them more agreeable to us. We nearly always assume that they don't have any feelings in that area. It won't bother them. We are quite willing to amputate anything in them which we find offensive. *I'll love you if - I'll accept you when - You can be a part of our group if* - and always what's implied is that something about you must be amputated because we don't like it. And we wonder why folks are suspicious, or give us the cold shoulder. Maybe they see that axe raised high in the air and they're not too sure of just what we're aiming for. *This won't hurt a bit, and we'll all be happier after*, somehow isn't much assurance either.

Don't Worry, Be Happy

I WAS WORKING OUTSIDE WHEN I remembered that I had promised a friend of mine that I would call him. Because I was dirty and sweaty, I went to the kitchen phone. When I picked it up, the line was dead, so I began searching the house for a phone with the receiver off the hook.

In the family room, the T.V. was on – but no one was in the room.

As I approached the kid's bedrooms, I felt the floors vibrating and observed that the wall hangings were swaying precariously. My daughter's stereo was blasting and on her bed there was a phone with the receiver off. All the lights were on, but there was no one there.

She was in the shower.

Your stereo is on, I screamed at the bathroom door. There was no response. I stuck my head in and I was almost suffocated by the steam. Through the fog I saw a red light glowing dimly and heard a high pitched hum. Her curling iron was on and her hair dryer was running. She was singing the words to some song I didn't know had words, but the refrain is,

Don't worry, be happy.

Your stereo is on, my voice was like a trumpet.

What? she says, *I can't hear you Dad - turn my stereo down -* and she sings - *Don't worry, be happy.*

I went and turned the stereo down, then came back, but I was not happy.

Kris, I said in a mild shout.

Don't yell, Dad, I can hear you, she says. *What do you want?*

Your stereo is on, I said with great intensity – less volume.

Yea, she says, *I know, now I can't hear it - turn it off will you? And Dad, while you're in the bedroom, would you see if Wendi is still on the phone? She wanted to listen to a tape of mine so I left the receiver off for her.*

Don't worry, be happy.

There is tension, frustration and unbelief in my voice. *I was trying to **use** the phone - and **you** left the receiver off for **Wendi** to listen to a song?*

Well, she's probably hung up by now - So you can use it if you like - Oh hey, Dad, have you seen my shoes? Don't Worry, Be Happy.

Oh hey, yourself, which pair are you looking for? There's one in every room. By the way, did you know the T.V. is on?

Yea, I'm watching a neat program. Don't Worry, Be Happy.

You're in the shower - you're not watching anything but steam - do you know how much it costs to heat water?

Relax, Dad, I'll be right out and I didn't want to have to wait for the picture tube to warm up.

Don't worry, be happy.

Did you know that your curling iron is on and your hair dryer is running?

Yea, I wanted them hot, when I got out. Don't worry, be happy. And hey Dad, could you leave me ten bucks to go out with my friends tonight?

Your iron and dryer are hot NOW! - and so am I!

Relax Dad, you're all tight.

Tight! Tight! - you think I'm tight! You haven't seen me tight, my precious - but you are going to see me tight! Tight - in my somewhat outdated vocabulary means - not free with money - you do understand money - right!

There was a very pronounced silence behind the shower curtain. I walked out softly, but as I moved down the hall, I couldn't refrain from singing - just loud enough to be heard,

Don't worry, be happy.

A Continual Dripping

*A quarrelsome wife is like
a constant dripping on a
rainy day; restraining her
is like restraining the wind or
grasping oil with the hand.*

Prov. 27:15-16

IN 1951 OR 52 MY FATHER bought a 1950 Buick. I remember it well because it was the car that I eventually learned to drive in. It had a *straight eight* motor and it was green. It was also huge. There was enough room in the back seat to put a kitchen table and chairs for people to sit and play cards. It must have weighed more than an elephant.

My mother was an excellent driver, but my dad drove whenever he was in the car. When mom drove, she was very calm and confident - when dad drove she was a nervous wreck (pun intended). She made little hissing noises when he turned corners, and she wore the carpet out and made indentations in the steel under her feet, pushing on the floorboard when he didn't apply the brakes fast enough to suit her. When he passed a car, she sort of moaned and writhed in her seat. She also gave him a steady stream of sound advice and helpful hints to keep him alert.

It never affected him much.

I guess that over the years he just *tuned her out* and drove pretty much like he wanted to. Occasionally – when she began to get on his nerves – he'd switch on the radio and raise the volume to a level appropriate to the decibels she was putting out. She was relentless, but my dad would keep his fingers on the volume control until she would have to give it up.

It sure brought the color to the back of her neck.

Much of the weather in Michigan is not conducive to safe driving. There is much fog, rain, snow, ice, and slush. We drove several miles to church and since the weather never interfered with our going – my dad drove in the worst of conditions.

From my back seat observation post, I witnessed much hissing, writhing, moaning, foot stomping and heard much conflicting advice:

> *Slow down, Fred!*
> *You're too close to the middle, Fred!*
> *Watch that car!*
> *Don't run off the edge!*
> *Go faster or we'll be late!*
> *Stop!*

And my dad drove on – completely impervious to her instructions and occasionally reaching for the radio knob. It was the best entertainment of every week and I always hoped the weather would be bad because good driving conditions sure took the fun out of going to church.

Although he never stopped her completely, he sure slowed her down some because of the following incident.

Driving under the type of weather conditions I mentioned earlier, inevitably leads to much slipping and sliding, especially with the road conditions of the fifties. Most of that slipping is completely harmless and people who drive in those conditions regularly, accept it and accommodate themselves to it quite naturally.

My mother read somewhere about a family that had lost control of their car and in the subsequent crash they had been trapped inside. When the car caught fire – they all burned to death. She developed a terrible psychotic paranoia about being trapped in a car. Every time our car slipped – even slightly – she would gasp, grab the door handle, open it and get ready to bail out if the car continued to slide.

No amount of reasoning could stop her.

One early spring night, we were returning home from church in Rochester in a wet, blinding snowstorm. My mother had stepped up both the quantity, quality, and volume of her advice and she was very tense. Somewhere between Square Lake Rd. and Sylvan Glen Golf Course, my dad lost control of the car. He wasn't going fast – there was no other traffic and we were in absolutely no danger at all. The big Buick began to spin slowly around and around in the road. It finally headed backwards and sideways toward the shallow ditch on the opposite side. Before we could stop her, my mother opened the door and bailed out. She slid ahead of the car, into the ditch and the Buick slid right over her.

My dad and I jumped out and ran to her assistance. She was completely unhurt, but quite uncomfortable, laying in the freezing water and wet snow. The Buick was right on top of her and we could not get her out. There simply was not room. We knew she was all right because we could still hear her muffled voice continuing her tirade about my dad's driving, and his failure to heed her good advice which was why she was where she was.

While she fumed, my dad and I discussed how best to extricate her. I thought we might try pushing the car forward and up the ditch bank, but my dad said that was no good because the bank might cave in. Then I suggested that we jack the car up high enough to make room to slide her out. My dad said that the jack would just sink in the mud. He said that he guessed we'd have to walk to town and get a wrecker that could lift the car. It was a long way to town and I wondered how mom was going to take the waiting, but I began to catch something in his voice and when I looked at him,

he winked at me.

We'll be back in no more than an hour Florence, he said, *You just rest easy.*

My mother had become extremely quiet during this last discussion, but now she spoke clearly.

Fred Smith, you get me out of here this minute, she said.

Well Florence, he said, *have you got any **advice** on how I might do that?*

The silence from under the car was broken only by the furious grinding of her mental wheels as they searched frantically for an answer.

No. she said.

Well, my dad said, in a very satisfied tone, *I just remembered that shovel I keep in the trunk to shovel snow at the church.*

He opened the trunk, got the shovel, and in ten minutes had made a hole big enough for her to crawl out.

She was a mess, soaking wet, freezing cold, covered with mud and quite miserable. My dad put his suit coat around her and we got into the comfortable warmth of the big Buick and drove home.

My mother gave no driving advice on the way home - in fact, she never recovered her old form. She never tried jumping out of the car again either, and whenever the car slipped she would move closer to my dad.

It sure did take the fun out of driving.

Obedience

Children, **obey** your parents

THE **FIRST** DUTY OF PARENTS is to teach **obedience**. Some might question that – saying that **loving** your children is first. My response would be that loving and obedience are inseparable, and that most of our problems in both areas can be traced to our attempts to treat them separately. The Bible never instructs parents to love their children but it does instruct them – many times

to **teach** obedience.

It is very important that you notice the word *teach* – because many parents only *enforce,* or *demand,* or *impose,* obedience – and that can be done, sometimes it is even necessary, but enforcing and imposing are only tools in the teaching process.

Obedience is our first relationship. Love comes **after** obedience – even as a **result** of it. Small children know little of love. The apostle John says, "we love *because* He first loved us," which means to me that love doesn't come first in our relationship with God either, it is the result of understanding His love. Children love only themselves, and **their** wants are more important than anybody else's. It's not their fault, it's simply the way of things. An infant is not concerned with his parent's finances, their rest, their schedule, their health or their mental condition – an infant is concerned with only **one thing** – its own comfort.

Until obedience is learned, no other lesson can be learned. It is a lesson which originates soon after birth. Parents who wait until their children are five or six are simply courting disaster. By that age the principle – the basic attitude of obedience must be deeply planted. If it is not, the next few years are going to be increasingly filled with pain and conflict – at home – at school – in the community.

The kind of obedience we're talking about is not grudging submission to a person who has the power to impose sanctions against you. It is not the foot dragging, sullen, resentful acquiescence of a subject to a tyrant. The obedience which God teaches - and which He expects us to both learn and teach our children is a willing - even happy relinquishing of our individual will to a loving wisdom that is recognized as being vastly superior to our own and is always acting in our best interests.

Teaching is a **process**. The finished product is the result of a long and difficult journey. Obedience is not taught in a day - it does not result from a lesson or a hundred lessons. It comes in stages and in years.

Children have totally different personalities. Some bend quickly and easily - even passively to instruction, and some are stubbornly rebellious. Teaching techniques must be constantly adjusted to accommodate the personality of the child.

My sister and I are perfect examples of the extremes of personality fluctuation. A sharply spoken reprimand from my parents absolutely crushed my sister - the slightest indication of displeasure or disappointment would reduce her to tears - to penitence - and to an immediate change in behavior. She really *wanted* to please, and - she took pleasure in doing so.

Words meant almost nothing to me - they glanced off me like bullets off of Superman - I was impervious to spoken instruction - it was the old, *in one ear - out the other* with me, nothing seemed to stick in between. My parents pleaded, reasoned and threatened. Only one thing got my attention - pain. I am very sorry to say it - but it is true. What **I** wanted to do took precedence over all other considerations. Even when I obeyed, it was more the result of my parent's plans meshing with my own, than submission. I took little pleasure in pleasing others, except when doing so pleased me. My obedience was a carefully measured balance between the joy I would get from doing what I wanted, and the pain I would suffer if I disobeyed.

My parents hated to give whippings - but since they were the only remedy to my affliction of disobedience - they took them seriously. Their theory was that one real good one had a more lasting effect than a dozen half hearted ones. I always knew exactly why I was receiving a whipping and although I dreaded them exceedingly, and would promise absolutely anything to avoid one - I do not ever remember receiving one that I thought was unjust. I never held it against them – never ran away from home, never entertained the notion. I liked my home – thought it was the greatest place in the world and couldn't conceive that anybody might have a better one.

I should explain that those were my *overall* feelings. I do not at all mean that I never had immediate or incidental resentments. Parents have to learn that children recover very quickly from punishment. That's why they repeat the unacceptable behavior so quickly after being punished for it. How many totally exasperated parents find themselves shouting, *I just punished you for this yesterday and two days before that, and last week – when are you going to learn not to do this?*

The gymnastics that parents go through – both oral, mental, and physical – trying to avoid having to administer corporal punishment are much more stressful on both them and the child than simply doing it. Why do parents punish themselves and lose their credibility in this way? Corporal punishment is a proven method, properly administered it works – it leaves no lasting scars or irreparable damage and most importantly, it has the divine stamp of approval on it.

Most parents have to sort of work their way up to it – like two junior high boys trying to work up a fight. Boys have to talk for several days, rumors must be spread, insults have to be traded, boasts must be made about the outcome, a crowd of supporters must be present, there has to be a great deal of pushing and shoving and of course they must make sure that there are adults in the area to break it up before anybody gets hurt.

The fight itself is anti-climatic
and so is the spanking.

Parents begin working themselves up to a spanking about the same way – they have to talk about it and threats have to be made –

If you do that seven more times I'll spank you.
Didn't I tell you that if you did that I'd spank you?
Did you hear me tell you that I'd spank you?
How many times do I have to tell you that I'll spank you for that?
I'll blister your bottom if you do that again.
Do you want me to spank you?

All of these threats of course, mean that the parent has absolutely no intention of <u>doing</u> any spanking at all – and the child knows that. Barking dogs do not bite – so the game goes on and the child establishes his superiority by conforming just enough to keep the string of threats going and no action taking place.

And parents wonder why they get no respect.

The method which seems most in vogue today is the counting method. I see it quite often and as a comedy routine it's hilarious – as a parenting method – it's sad. This is how it goes:

Step One: Father and friend are standing in backyard visiting – child wanders off toward the street and father is on duty so he warns the child not to go farther.

Step Two: Child takes a few more steps and father repeats warning telling the child to return. Child stops but does not return.

Step Three: Father repeats instructions – a little louder – and returns to conversation with friend – child stands and stares at Father.

Step Four: Child takes a few more steps toward the street, stops to make sure father is looking, and Father raises voice again. *Did you hear what I said?* Child is not deaf, because he stops – but does not return. The battle intensity increases noticeably because the Father is now under pressure because of the friend. *Get back here!*

Step Five: Child stands and stares, then sits down. Father starts counting. One and two come very fast, then he realizes that he hasn't established the rules for the game i.e., when the count ends. *I want you back here before I reach five.* Of course he starts the count over with one, which takes the pressure off.

Step Six: Child sits and stares: *two, three* – again there is a pause as father realizes that he hasn't told the child what he's going to do if the five count is reached and the child hasn't responded. "If you're not back here by the time I count five, I'll spank you."

Step Seven: Child sits and stares. The count starts over, "One – two – three," "Did you hear what Daddy said?" The father is pleading now; he may actually have to do some- thing. He starts again at "two" – long pause and no response: "three" – even longer pause and no response:"four," Father is sweating, child looks at father to see how serious he is and realizes his dad is in a bind. He knows he's already won the contest and established his superiority, so he takes three steps in his father's direction, thereby establishing a new basis for continuing the game. He's having the time of his life at the national pastime called, "parent baiting." The game is played in homes, supermarkets, parks and automobiles, millions of times every day much to the amusement and satisfaction of children.

The whole idea behind genuine obedience is that it is not incidental but attitudinal. Teaching obedience is done by consistently demanding it – and demonstrating it – by which I mean that parents must show that they too live under authority – that they obey the rules, both civil, social and spiritual– and by enforcing it over an extended period of time until it becomes a part of the mental framework – not something associated with specific instruction.

I must not leave this critical area of instruction without adding this note. I do not remember exactly when – but somewhere about my twelfth or thirteenth year my parents stopped whipping me. My father very purposefully and carefully explained to me that that time was over and that from now on he would deal differently with me. I believe he was absolutely right. He recognized that our relationship and my understanding of obedience had to be raised to a higher level –

a level of conscious reflection and reasoned response.

The first step in our relationship with God is a **recognition** of authority which must lead to **obedience**. That is the lesson that Adam and Eve did not grasp – if they had, all would be different. The history of Israel – of mankind – is a history of disobedience and what the consequences of disobedience are. No other aspect of our relationship to parents, to society, or to God can be developed without first learning – to obey.

As a parent, a preacher, a counselor, a teacher, a coach and a friend – I solemnly warn you.

There is no substitute for obedience

Though He was a Son,

Yet learned He *obedience*

By the things that He *suffered*.

Heb. 5:8

163

He Who Spares the Rod

THE PLAY, *THE MIRACLE WORKER,* is the story of the life of Helen Keller - a blind, deaf and speechless girl who ultimately becomes an accomplished author and public speaker. It is also the story of Anne Sullivan, who helped Helen Keller to become a legend in the area of overcoming handicaps.

Because of her physical liabilities, Helen is badly spoiled by her misguided and indulgent parents. She becomes an intolerable nuisance - a useless burden to her family and to herself. When Anne Sullivan is hired to train and teach Helen, she meets with peevish, sullen rebellion. When Anne attempts to discipline Helen by imposing restrictions and punishing unacceptable behavior, Helen's parents rush to defend their daughter. The major turning point in Helen's life is when Anne Sullivan confronts Helen's parents with this ultimatum. *Helen must first learn to **obey** me -*
until she does, I can teach her nothing.

The same lesson is applicable to so many areas of our lives. As a public school teacher, I learned quickly that it was more important for students to obey me, than to like me. Parents left their children with me to teach them - and they, like Helen Keller's parents, had often already rendered them unsuitable for any kind of learning, because they had not taught them the first lesson - the preschool lesson that comes before the association of letters and sounds -
the lesson of obedience.

A few months ago I was trying to make my way through the Atlanta Airport. My schedule was tight, not critical, but I had no time to waste. At one point I came to an impasse in the walkway, an absolute bottleneck. After much maneuvering, I finally arrived at the obstruction. A youngster of about eight or nine had parked his suitcase, with himself on top of it, and refused to go further. If you had taken a measuring tape and determined the exact width of the aisle, divided it in two on a calculator which would take it to the seventeenth decimal point, you could not have found the exact center with any more precision. His mother, teary eyed and embarrassed, had also parked her belongings and was on her knees in front of him, pleading with him to move.

I have no idea what caused him to balk. I did learn that his name was Danny, but I listened to his mother grovel and beg and apologize and promise and reason with him until I was absolutely sick. And while she pleaded, the traffic stacked up behind them on every side.

A rather large man, wearing a western hat and cowboy boots, offered with some degree of enthusiasm to move him for her, but she would not allow him to be *forced* because it *upset him* too much. *Force,* the man said with two very descriptive expletives, *Lady, I'm not going to use force, I'm going to boot his fanny all the way to the end of the runway and he can sit there as long as he wants!* But Danny didn't care about other people, or his mother, or plane schedules, or anything else, but Danny. He was enjoying his rule asking for a day.

I felt sorry for the mother. She was pitiful. She was very smartly dressed, her hair was beautifully done and I assume that her makeup had been as flawless as the rest of her appearance - now it was all over her face. I felt sorry for the people who were inconvenienced, I felt sorry for myself because the incident soured my stomach and for several hours thereafter ruined an otherwise pleasurable trip: I felt sorry for Danny's school teachers - for his future wife - even for his future children, and I even felt sorry for Danny because-
I know what's in store for him.

Danny faces a lifetime of frustration, disappointment and disillusionment. The world will soon stop bowing to his whims. There will be toys too large for his mother's purse - there will be laws which must be obeyed - and Danny will learn the lesson of obedience in a very cruel world, and Danny will suffer and he will bring suffering to everyone around him.

Danny might have learned obedience in a loving, caring atmosphere, and he might have learned it in areas of little consequence, but his parents chose to spare themselves that pain and so now he will learn in a very tough school and both he and his parents will suffer for their neglect.

If I could have asked this mother where this began, I'm sure she would have had no idea - but I could tell her. It began with Danny in his high chair throwing his toys on the floor and gleefully watching his mother retrieve them time after time like a faithful puppy. It began with her reading about interfering with a child's independence - that somehow a child would naturally see the "reasonableness" of obedience. It began before he could walk, when he reached for something and she said *no* and then said it again and again - but *no* didn't mean anything. It began when he was a toddler and his mother told him to pick up his toys - but he preferred not to - so she picked them up and she has been picking up his toys ever since. And now, here she was on her knees in the aisle of the Atlanta airport begging her son to move –

and she didn't know why.

God says:

> *He who spares the rod,*
> *hates his son.*
> *But he who loves him,*
> *disciplines him promptly.*

Who do we have our confidence in – twentieth century psychologists who have been studying behavior for twenty years and write books about behavior modification – people who either have no children or whose children are woeful examples of their parents' misguided philosophy? Or do we have confidence in the God who created us, and who has left timeless instructions for us to follow?

Wet Feet

ONE OF MY BESETTING SINS as a youngster was getting my feet wet. I was a child of the ditches, ponds and streams. Wherever there were snakes, tadpoles, frogs, crayfish or minnows I was never far away. We did not wear boots in those day, we wore *galoshes*. Oh my, you don't know galoshes do you? They were boots, calf-high, black boots that you put your whole shoe down inside of, and then buckled them up. Actually, my problem with wet feet was not my fault at all. The problem was that the people who made galoshes didn't understand boys very well, and consequently never built them tall enough, or with the fronts higher than the backs, so that when your leg tilted forward the water wouldn't run in.

My mother soon grew weary of my coming home with wet feet and started whipping me on each occasion. Not meeting with any significant success, she soon pressured my father into this plot against me, and he whipped me also. I am ashamed to admit that I was a very slow child and receiving two whippings per occasion only slowed me down a very little.

You may wonder why having wet feet constituted such a serious problem? A major part of it was economics. The water ruined the inside of my galoshes and caused my shoes to decay. Galoshes and shoes cost money - money was very scarce, and besides it was wasteful,

and to waste was ungodly.

You must understand that I did not mean to get my feet wet. It was just that whatever I was trying to catch inevitably got into water which was slightly higher than my galoshes. When I felt that icy trickle and the creeping wetness in my socks, I was absolutely sick, I knew what awaited me. When I got home, I walked stiff legged on my heels, so my shoes wouldn't squish, but my mother always noticed my peculiar gait. She would say,

John, stand on your heels.

Yes, ma'am.

Now rock forward on your toes.

Yes, ma'am - the tell tale squish was devastating.

Do you have wet feet?

Yes, ma'am.

It was whipping time again.

You must understand that I hated whippings, dreaded them. You must not think that by whipping I mean some quiver lipped, weak kneed, half-hearted, apologetic, backhanded swat on the rear. No sir! I mean a pull your pants down, bend over that chair, knotty apple tree branch, down to business, bottom-buster that raised quarter inch welts and motivated one toward sobriety and repentance with loud cries and tears. I always solemnly promised myself that I would-

never get my feet wet again.

I don't know how long this went on. My mother vowed that it lasted three years, resulted in two hundred odd whippings, and ruined two fine apple trees.

I always thought that was an exaggeration.

My father grew weary of this merry-go-round. On one occasion, before he whipped me, he expressed this with some heat. *I'm getting sick and tired of spanking you for wet feet,* he said. It was the best news I'd had in some time, since it was beginning to tell on me also. I interpreted his statement to mean he was going to quit. It just goes to show how mortally mistaken a person can be - because he proceeded to give me a whipping which made all the others pale into insignificance. He was in a considerable passion when he started and it seemed that the longer it lasted, the more involved he became. When he finished I hurt too much to even cry - the only time I can remember - but I promise you that he had my attention. It worked.

I stopped getting my feet wet.

Parents who fail to teach their children that unacceptable behavior has painful consequences, are failing to prepare them for the real world and even more importantly, for a right relationship with God. Sometimes parents need to *get serious* with their children

to get their *attention.*

Discipline

MY COUSIN DANIEL WAS THE youngest of five children. He was raised in a house which closely resembled a cross between a three-ring circus and a Salvation Army Center. We went there often, because his mother was my mother's youngest sister, and my mother genuinely tried to help her. My aunt should never have had children. She was a pleasant woman, quick to laugh, or cry, and I liked her very much, but she had no discipline. She had none for herself, and none for her family, even I could see that. My uncle was a fine, hard working man, but he was no help at all.

I never ceased to be amazed at the absolute chaos which characterized their home. Meals were never scheduled, laundry, at all stages of going and coming, was lying everywhere, the screens were loose or torn, the shades wouldn't pull, and there always seemed to be a certain feeling of impending disaster hanging in the atmosphere. The kids knew they could get away with anything. When they committed some major infraction and my aunt got stirred up, she would grab a fly swatter and begin to chase them. Around the dining room table they would go, jumping chairs, knocking over lamps, with her in hot pursuit, waving her fly swatter. Then she would get tired and she could see how ridiculous she was and it tickled her. She would collapse in a chair, all in a heap and she would laugh until she cried.

That was discipline at my aunt's house.

Danny was a handsome boy, with a pleasant personality. He and I were pretty close for awhile. He had a flaming temper, and he was quick to lie. He was often in trouble; at first in the neighborhood, then at school, and finally with the authorities. He was never disciplined at home. He was given every conceivable gift, things his parents simply could not afford.

When Danny's problems began to get serious, and other problems in his home occurred simultaneously, he came to stay with us. I believe his parents hoped that with the heavier hand of my father, Danny would do better. He did. He honestly improved some, but just when it seemed he might really pull out, he would be jerked out of our home. It was never long until he was in trouble again.

My father was very kind to him, and very understanding too, but he punished him severely for recalcitrance. On one occasion, the last time he came to us, he took some money from my mother's purse. He was accustomed to doing it at home with no fear of reprisal. We were in the living room when my father confronted him. He lied, and said he hadn't done it. My father told him that he was going to give him one more chance to be a man and face up to his guilt, but Danny was too steeped in his old ways, and he little understood my father, *No,* he said again, *I didn't take it.* My father told him he was going to be punished for lying and stealing. I think Danny had some notion of maybe missing supper or being confined to his room. You cannot imagine how confused he looked, when my father told him to get up and go outside with him. *What are we going to do?* he asked. – I could have told him. *I'm going to whip you, and you're going to be sorry,* my father replied.

Danny had never been whipped, and his lack of understanding of my father led him to an even greater mistake; he refused to get up, and sat clinging to the arms of his chair. "Daniel," my father's voice was dangerously quiet – *you can either walk outside, or be carried outside – chair and all – I'm getting mad, and that's not good for you.*

I was terrified and I wasn't even involved. I wanted to tell Danny that the best possible solution was to excuse himself, go to the bathroom and cut his throat, but I knew better than to speak. They went outside, Danny walked, and my father whipped him. I could hear the whistling cracks of the switch and his cries – my whole body squirmed and ached in sympathy with his.

He improved, he honestly did. Then he left again, and I didn't see him for some time. One day, I overheard my parents talking about him being sent to a juvenile detention center.

During his stay there he ran away twice. Do you know where he went when they were hunting for him? Did he return home where he had never been punished or reproved? No! He came to us, both times. He came late at night. He came to the only place that had brought order to his disordered life, the only place where lines were clearly drawn and he had been punished for crossing them.

I felt so sorry for him. He would be thin and worn, poorly dressed and scared. He was still only just a boy and life was hard on him. My father always allowed him to stay a while and they talked much. We fed him, clothed him, but since he was a fugitive he must go back. He would plead with my father, vowing to change his ways, and he meant it too.

But it could not be.

Daniel suffered. He suffered for his parent's sins, and for his own as well. The Hebrew author asks us, *What son is there whom his father does not discipline?* The answer to that question is obvious, *an unloved son.* Scripture tells us plainly that God disciplines us. It is an integral part of His love. We are even told that God's discipline brings sorrow, the implication is that it may be severe in nature. He does it **that**, *we may share His holiness.* God's purpose in discipline is never punitive, it is always corrective and instructive and our motives must be the same.

That is the only purpose for discipline,
altered behavior.

Though He Was A Son

*Though He was a Son, yet He learned obedience
by the things which He suffered.* Heb. 5:8

THE PORTERS LIVED ABOUT A quarter of a mile west of us. Their house sat way back off the road and was almost totally hidden by huge old maples and elms. It was sort of a forbidding old place and the neighborhood kids did not cross their property. Mrs. Porter was a step back in time with her floor length dresses and her bonnets and shawls. I saw her often, working in her flowers, shrubs, and garden. She was always stooped over or on her knees. I thought she didn't like me much.

She never smiled or spoke.

At the time I am concerned with, my father had bought me a great present, something almost beyond value, a Buck Jones, pump action, B.B. gun. When he gave it to me, he was very serious and he warned me sternly about its proper use. He gave me a specific list of birds that I could shoot - starlings, blackbirds, grackles and sparrows. I was to kill no songbirds, blue jays or cardinals. I was so excited I paid little attention I fear, but when he asked if I understood, I said yes and promised to obey.

One morning I killed a blackbird (actually it was a grackle) sitting on the telephone wires in front of the Porter's house. I went over to inspect my prey, and that feeling of shame, which always confused and irritated me when I killed a bird, came over me. I was standing there, alone with my thoughts, when Mrs. Porter appeared. I hadn't seen her because she was hidden by her lilac bushes. When I say *appeared,* you must understand that I mean that literally. One moment I was alone, the next moment she was there - not there as in thirty feet - but there, as in two feet. She absolutely scared me speechless. I thought she was a wraith, with her bonnet down over her face and her loose garments flapping in the wind. *What did you shoot?* she demanded in a very accusing tone! *A starling,* I stammered. The bird was lying right at my feet. Mrs. Porter lifted my face to hers by my chin and said, *You dumb boy, that's no starling, that's a grackle, and lucky for you.*

Don't you ever kill any song birds near my place!

About two-three weeks went by. I was going to see my friend, Doug Bussey, who lived next door to the Porters. It was a pretty, sunny, June day, tailor-made for a nine year old boy. I was barefoot, tanned and looking for adventure. Sitting on the telephone wire in front of the Porters, singing his heart out, was a yellow breasted canary. There were many warning voices saying, *No,* but there was another voice, stronger than my father's warning, stronger than Mrs. Porter's imprecations, the voice of what I wanted to do - and I shot the canary. Oh, I told myself I was just going to scare it - but I killed it deader than a hammer. I looked around quickly - certain that Mrs. Porter would descend upon me from some unseen quarter, but no one came. I went on my way quickly, conscience-stricken, leaving behind me the tiny, unoffending body of a song bird.

It was two days later. With absolutely no introduction or explanation, my father told me that we were going to the Porters that evening after supper. Even my mother was going. We had never been to the Porters before and there could be only one reason for going now.

I was terrified.

I still remember the walk to the Porters. My father and mother walked rather rapidly, with firmness and resolution, they did not talk. Normally, I would have been running ahead, making side excursions, showing off, but on this night I slunk along behind, dreading the termination of our journey.

I remember that the house was large. The ceilings in the rooms were much higher than ours and the things on the walls were ornate and looked expensive to my unpracticed eye. Everything looked old and fragile. With my natural propensity for breaking things, I was scared to move. The room we sat in was painfully clean, neat, orderly. I sat in a chair much too large for me and I was most uncomfortable.

After the initial courtesies had passed, my father informed me that Mrs. Porter had seen me shoot the canary. Since I had broken my word to him, and since I had openly showed disrespect for Mrs. Porter, I must be punished and we were here to determine how I could best repay Mrs. Porter and demonstrate my penitence. My father was very severe in his manner and I knew that he was deeply hurt and disappointed by my conduct. I was genuinely penitent and began to cry, not just because I had hurt my father, but also, I must admit, I knew that what was in store for me was not going to be pleasant.

Mrs. Porter got up and came to where I was sitting and stood by my chair. I guess I'd never looked at her before - I mean really seen her. She always looked like a large woman but actually she was very small. I guess it was her loose, baggy clothing that had made me think her large. She was bent and crooked and her white hair was thin and wispy. Her face was pinched and wrinkled and not at all unpleasant, just old. She told me she had a lot of yard work she wanted done and that after I had done some for the bird, she would pay me for the rest. But, she added, there was one other condition which absolutely must be met. I had visions of my Buck Jones broken into pieces. I was not prepared at all, neither were my folks, for the condition she named.

A few weeks earlier, my parents had invited their church friends to our house for watermelon and singing. About sixty or seventy had come. We had sung out by the grape arbor until very late at night. We did not know it, but the Porters had heard us and had walked down the road and listened for some time. The final condition of my probation was that I must sing for Mrs. Porter.

When we got home two things happened. My father and I went outside. He told me that I was to work hard for Mrs. Porter and that any report of the slightest refractory behavior on my part would lead to the most serious consequences. I begged him to not make me go to the Porter's. I even told him I would take a whipping (you simply cannot know what a concession that was) but he was absolutely implacable. To make matters worse, he told me that I was going to receive a whipping anyway, because I had broken my word. I still remember the pain in his voice as he told me what a serious sin I had committed. He explained that our total relationship was based on trust and when that trust was violated we could never be sure of each other. I know I didn't understand all he said, but I understood very well that folks who broke their word, who didn't keep their commitments were pretty much useless.

When I went to bed that night, still smarting from the whipping I had received, I believe I was aware of alienation for the first time. Oh, I didn't call it that, I had no name for it at all, but I knew that my father hadn't come to my room to say goodnight to me, and that what I had done had separated us somehow.

For the next three weeks, except Sundays, I trooped to the Porter's at daylight and Mrs. Porter, and occasionally Mr. Porter and I worked in the shrubs and garden. At first the work was drudgery, the singing was hard; I couldn't think of songs, but gradually, one song would remind me of another, and sometimes she would ask me to repeat one. After two or three days, Mrs. Porter began to hum bits and pieces and sing a word now and then. All in all, it wasn't too bad. Mrs. Porter would fix lunch for us and we would talk. I learned they had no children. When my time of confinement was up we parted, but ever after we were friends and the Porter house was no longer forbidding to me – but friendly and I seldom passed without a smile or a *hello*.

The last week, my father would be waiting for me when I finished my work. I would see him talking to Mr. Porter. We would walk home together. Sometimes he would tell me about his job, (it was wartime and he worked at the tank arsenal), sometimes we would just walk quietly. It was his way of saying that everything was all right and that I was forgiven.

I was always grateful for his company.

The Hebrew author tells us in 2:10 that God thought it was fitting to perfect Jesus, the author of our salvation, through suffering. He also states in 5:6 that He (Jesus) learned obedience from the things he suffered. How tragic it is, that our society is unwilling to allow its children to suffer until such time as obedience is not what is learned - only rebellion and anger. Our children are raised as painlessly as possible, until those inevitable times come when we can no longer physically, financially, or emotionally shield or rescue them. And we wonder why they lack self-discipline, character, sensitivity and moral fiber.

Those things are only learned in one way.

What marvelous lessons I learned as a boy. God must have a special place in His great heart for mischievous boys who must always learn hard. I thank God daily for my father, a kind, tender, compassionate man who could be stern and strong and absolutely unbending when the occasion arose. And I thank God for the Porters and what I learned there. I have never, not till this very day, ever killed another song bird. You see, my father not only taught me **obedience**, he taught me "piety"-

a feeling of deep respect
for all of God's creation.

He prayeth best, who loveth best
all creatures, great and small.

Sorrow Without Regret

FOR THE SORROW THAT IS *according to the will of God, produces a repentance without regret.* 2 Cor. 7:10

It wasn't much of an outhouse –
but it was the only one we had.

It stood about six feet from the back of the chicken coop – old, gray, weathered, and large. It was a *two holer,* with enough room left over for my dad to store bales of hay. It was about thirty yards from the house. I hated the trip – especially when it was dark and particularly especially when it was dark and winter. The shadowy night with the sounds of the wind in the trees – the rustling rats who lived in the hay bales, the swooping bats and hooting owls, the eerie, drifting noises of the night creatures of the swamp – the cold, hard seat – the dark opening that might hold spiders or wasps or worse – all combined to make me draw my knees up under my chin, hold it, and pray to God to please let the sun come up.

Our house, and the outhouse, sat on a hill which overlooked the swamp, where grew millions of cattails. In late summer they ripened – and not only did they look like long, fat cigars – when properly lit – they smoldered like cigars – and smelled ten times better. Some folks gathered and lit them because the smoke drove off the mosquitoes.

James and I lit them
just for the fun of it.

On one occasion, we had cut hundreds of them and we were lighting them as rapidly as possible. Some were still green and they burned very reluctantly. This was not to be tolerated, so we stuck them down the long-necked kerosene can – that my father also stored in the outhouse – and soaked them. After that, they burned spectacularly and we thought we were very clever.

James had just soaked one – apparently pretty thoroughly – because the excess kerosene ran down the stalk and onto his hand. As he came out of the outhouse, I was going in. My burning cattail touched his unlit one and ignited it – the flames raced down the stalk and onto his hand. His immediate reaction was to throw the cattail – and he did – right into the hay bales. The resulting conflagration was breathtaking – we stood in absolute awe, as the old, dry, weather beaten outhouse went up in flames.

My mother came out – in a state of some excitement – and frantically tried to organize an effort to put it out. She tried to enlist

James and me, but her directions were often confusing and truth-fully our efforts were less than half-hearted. Every time we went for a bucket of water – which had to pumped by hand – we missed some of the excitement – besides, even a child could see that it was hopeless. It was amazing how quickly the whole thing collapsed and fell sizzling – right into the hole over which it had stood for so many years.

I wasn't sorry to see it go – until I thought of how my father would react when he got home. I was pretty sure he wouldn't be too happy with the afternoon's activities. When he pulled into the driveway, I was on the front porch with my mother. Normally, I would have met him at the road and raced alongside the car as he pulled up to the house – but not today –

today I stood behind my mother.

He knew something was wrong right off, and he knew that it involved me – because it always did. *What happened?* he said. *John burned down the outhouse,* she said, with no preliminary at all. That really upset me because she didn't say that James had actually done it and I just happened to be there – she made it sound like I had deliberately set fire to it – she left out that it was an accident. *What?* my father said. It wasn't the kind of *what,* that means that you didn't understand or hear – it was the kind of *what,* that signifies amazement or disbelief. Slowly, carefully, she repeated, *John – burned – down – the – outhouse.* It was like – *read my lips,* and again she left James out.

My dad put his lunch pail down on the front porch and he walked around the corner of the house with my mother and I walking behind. You know how sometimes you want something so badly that you believe it's true? Well, I wanted that outhouse to be there so badly when we turned that corner that I thought it would be – I mean it had always been there, why shouldn't it be there now – maybe God had put it back when I wasn't looking – but He hadn't–

it was definitely gone.

We went into the house. My mother explained now in some detail what had happened – and this time she included James – which was a great relief to me – except somehow James didn't come out looking quite as bad as he would have if I had told the story. I had not said a word. When my mother finished, he was very quiet, then he said that he would go up to see Mr. Macfarland after supper.

He didn't have to. Mr. Macfarland and James came down to our house and the two of them stood out close to where the outhouse had been and talked quietly for quite a while. When they finished, they called James and me over and told us what they had decided. Our punishment would be that we would dig the hole for the new outhouse by hand, with spades. The dirt from the new hole would fill the old one. They laid out the dimensions with stakes, and the next day we began.

We suffered. It is no exaggeration – we really did. We stayed at it from early morning to late evening – two boys, eight or nine years old – digging a hole, eight feet deep, four feet wide, and eight feet long. We handed up dirt in buckets when the hole was over our heads.

I was bitterly resentful toward what seemed to me unjust treatment. My injured pride and my rebellious anger made me sullen and withdrawn. *James had thrown the cattail,* I reasoned, *Why should I be punished for his stupidity?* I thought my father the most heartless, unjust tyrant that ever lived.

I would not speak unless forced to.

I am sure my father wavered. He probably often questioned the wisdom of his decision, but he saw it through.

The night we finished, he came to my room after supper. I had gone there directly after eating, to nurse my wrongs. He stood in the doorway. He quietly complimented me on doing a good job and staying with a very difficult assignment.

He said he was proud of me.

I was so tired, I felt so wronged, I was so angry – and I was only just a boy. When I could restrain myself no longer – I began to speak – to pour out my resentment in a jumbled torrent, which ended with hot tears streaming down my face. My father stood quietly, his broad shoulders slightly stooped, and pain written in every line of his face. I ended my tirade by rushing to him and burying my face in his shirt – I threw my arms around him and sobbed. *I'm sorry, Dad. I'm sorry –*

and I really was, you know.

I know now, how it must have lifted his heavy heart. I know now how he must have felt, when he tucked me in and turned out the light. His sorrow and mine were without regret.

> *For the sorrow that is according to*
> *the will of God,*
> *Produces a repentance...*
> *Without regret...*

CHAPTER
10

Parenting and Happiness

There is only one way to achieve happiness
on this terrestrial ball. That is -
To have either a clear conscience -
Or - none at all.

Ogden Nash

MOST PARENTS ARE TERRIBLY concerned with their children's happiness. Few things strike more deeply into a parent's heart than a tear-streaked face or a dejected, defeated, crestfallen countenance. I suspect that potential happiness has more influence on parental decision making than any other factor. The decision to buy or do something because it will make your child *happy* - defeats any practical argument to the contrary. Interestingly enough, it is the one major quality that is totally absent from divine instruction. That's right, God never charges parents with responsibility for making their children *happy*.

Happiness is an abstract quality and definitions are hard to pin down. Happiness is a feeling - an emotion which seems to result from satisfactory conclusions. Ideas of happiness change with age and environmental circumstances, but let me try to give some working definitions for my purposes.

For most of us, happiness is equated with positive results, ie; I win, I get the girl, the pay raise, the bicycle, the biggest fish, the promotion - the green light, and that makes me *happy*. Being happy due to positive results is very tenuous however, because often - no matter how hard we try - the results are negative - which can only mean unhappiness.

Parents get caught up in trying to guarantee positive results. They spend themselves, supplying the means to achieve those positive results until either their financial ability or personal influence is inadequate – the inevitable *crash* disillusions both them and their children.

A second source of happiness is *being* – ie, being popular, being powerful – being pretty or handsome – being talented, musically, athletically, oratorically, dramatically – being brilliant – being tall – or being rich. Once again, parents ability to supply happiness on this level is extremely limited and initial successes lead only to disaster.

A third source of happiness is in *wanting* and in *anticipation* of *getting,* there is probably more downright happiness in imagining, than in *having.* The moment that our wants are realized, and *getting* takes place, happiness goes into decline until new wants arise. There is no physical reality that can live up to its anticipation. That is why happiness is not only illusive but impossible, as our society has defined it. And that is also why parents can do so little to help their children to actualize their happiness.

When we are small we want to be adults. We want to be grown up and enjoy all that we anticipate the grown up world to be. But when we arrive, we learn all too soon that being an adult isn't all its cracked up to be. The *reality* of the adult world does not measure up to the *anticipation* of it – so we flee from that reality – ultimately seeking joy in trying to recapture our youth – which is another unreality.

Even if we take Nash's criteria of happiness – as the result of the condition of a person's conscience, we can readily see that parents cannot supply either *clear* consciences or *no* consciences.

When children are small, I suppose the thing they want most in order to be happy is to have their way. It is not the drink, or the teddy bear, or the light in the hallway, or to go to the bathroom – that they want, no – it is that they want to be, *in control.* And for a while at least, you can give them that – that is until they go to school – until they must confront a neighborhood or a society which is totally unsympathetic with their whims.

My point is that happiness cannot be supplied directly, and that parents who use happiness as a criteria for their success are doomed to constant failure. Stop trying to make your children happy! You cannot do it! You can teach them diligence, and even honesty and sharing–

but you cannot teach them happiness.

Happiness is a by-product – I think Nash has it right, it has to be **discovered**. In his estimation it is a by-product of the state of your conscience – which is a good place to start. Think about that.

Happiness, which is achieved from a *clear* conscience, is happiness based upon **living in a morally responsible way** – the consequence of doing your duty or following a clearly outlined standard of principles.

Happiness achieved by having *no* conscience, is the sensual gratification we experience when we get what we want without regard to the means we used to obtain it or the potential outcomes.

God never tells us to be happy. He tells us to take up our cross and follow – to do our duty – and He promises that peace will result. Let me note some Bible references to illustrate the fact that happiness is the by-product – often of the most peculiar things.

1. Job 5:17 – happiness is the **result** of God's correction.
2. Prov. 14 – happiness **results** from helping the poor.
3. Ps. 128 – happiness is the **result** of physical labor.
4. Prov. 16 – happiness **results** from trusting in God.
5. Jn. 13 – happiness **results** from serving others – washing feet.
6. I Pet. 3:14 – happiness **results** from suffering for righteousness.
7. I Pet. 4:14 – happiness **results** from being reproached for Jesus' sake.

Children can lay an incredible load of guilt on parents by blaming them for their unhappiness. Parents who have mistakenly accepted that responsibility are doomed to flagellate themselves for their failure. The result is, that parents obligate themselves to a type of happiness which is inevitably *short term,* and has the seeds of unhappiness woven into it. Christian parents cannot and must not preserve their children from suffering. It can only be postponed – never eliminated – and every postponement increases the depth and longevity of the inevitable.

Happiness needs to be redefined in the light of inspired principles. Parents have labored too long under the burden of a cultural definition, to which Christianity not only offers no solution, but seems to stand in direct opposition. In the cultural sense of happiness – we would be much *happier* if we were not Christians.

In the same way, Christian parents have accepted a culturally oriented obligation to make their children happy, an obligation which is not from God and,

which only leads,

to emptiness.

Daisy

I HAD A TWO HOUR LAY-OVER in Dallas. I parked myself in an out-of-the-way corner because I had reading to do and did not wish to be disturbed. I was reading, actually rereading - *The Great Gatsby*, F. Scott Fitzgerald's magnificent description of the shallowness, extravagance and excess of *The Roaring Twenties*. I was using it as a text for an American Novel class I was teaching. Fitzgerald's female heroine is named *Daisy*. How many *Daisy's* do you know? In all of my teaching and preaching career, spanning thirty-five years, and ten states, I have never met nor heard of a female named *Daisy*, with the exception of a ridiculous song I used to hear my mother sing - which went something like this -

> *Daisy, Maisie, give me your answer true.*
> *I'm half crazy, all for the love of you.*
> *It won't be a stylish marriage*
> *I can't afford a carriage,*
> *But you'll look sweet, upon the seat,*
> *Of a bicycle built for two.*

There are no areas of the Dallas Airport where a person is totally alone, but I had found one with relatively few people. On my left, about ten seats away, was a young oriental boy - sipping a coke and reading intently. To my right, seven or eight seats away, was a young mother with a two or three year old daughter. There were a few scattered businessmen with the inevitable briefcase - as much a part of their dress as the dark suit, white shirt, black shoes and loosened tie, by which they maintain their identity.

What follows is a blow by blow description of events. I became so intrigued that I actually took out my notebook and recorded them as they happened. I am often guilty of embellishment, exaggeration and the addition of *color*. In this case the actual facts are quite sufficient.

I was reasonably well *settled in,* when the young mother called the little girl to come back to her seat, *Daisy,* she cried, *Come back here.* I had Fitzgerald's book right in my hand - it was incredible. I became fascinated by *Daisy* and her mother. The child was dressed beautifully, very ornately, with frilly and elaborate clothing, but her shoes had been removed. The mother was dressed very casually and she had also removed her shoes. Daisy was bored and wandered restlessly around the area. The first three chases I witnessed were simply the routine type when Daisy wandered too far, or threatened the peace of other travelers. Each chase was preceded by the mother calling, first pleading, then coaxing, then threatening. Daisy was oblivious. Her mother might as well have been whistling the proverbial *Dixie.* Meeting no success with her threats, she would heave herself to her feet, chase Daisy down, catch her and bring her back, kicking -

struggling and screaming.

Chase number four began when Daisy spit a piece of candy on the carpet. The mother told her to pick it up - Daisy preferred not to and stood in open defiance. Eventually the mother came and picked it up - much to Daisy's satisfaction - and asked her if she wanted another piece. After four repetitions of the question, Daisy agreed to take one but she insisted that her mother place it in her mouth. When she obediently complied, Daisy bit her fingers, apparently quite hard, because her mother gasped - then screamed. As she stood, first shaking her injured fingers, then placing them in her own mouth, Daisy laughed, then ran and -

chase number five ensued.

Daisy's next excursion was in my direction. Out of the corner of my eye I saw her coming. She was taking her time, whacking each intervening seat with her fist, but I was definitely the objective. She really was cute. She whacked the seat beside me and then paused, right in front of me, chubby little fist raised high in a threatening position, waiting for my response. I ignored her. She wasn't used to it - she tapped me on the knee - I ignored her - she tapped harder and made little gurgly baby noises, demanding me to pay attention - I ignored her. She stepped on my toe as hard as she could. She had no shoes on and it didn't hurt -

but it made me mad -

and sad.

Is she bothering you? The mother's voice inquired.

Yes, I said, *but not as you mean it.*

She looked at me - and was about to express her bewilderment when she was interrupted by a scream. Daisy had spotted another child, some distance away, who had a small stuffed animal. With no hesitation, she snatched the stuffed animal from the unsuspecting child and started toward her mother. Her scream of indignation, was prompted when the child tried to recapture the toy. Daisy, realizing that her mother was not on her side, turned and ran down the main aisle - chase number six was in progress. The mother brought her back to the area, pleading with her to surrender the animal and finally, by sheer physical strength wrenched it from Daisy's death grip - damaging the toy in the process, while

Daisy screamed bloody murder.

The mother now paraded up and down in front of the huge plate glass windows overlooking the plane refueling and parking area, pointing to everything of interest to distract Daisy's attention from her recent setback. She partially succeeded - to the great relief of everyone in the area. Worn out - she returned to a seat somewhat closer to me than previously. Embarrassed, apologetic, obviously frustrated, she said, *I just can't wait till she gets a little older so I can begin disciplining her.*

It will soon be entirely too late, I said.

Oh, do you think so? she asked with interest.

I know so, I said.

She wanted to ask something else, but she noticed that Daisy had taken one of her shoes and made off with it. *Come back here,* she called, and there was genuine anger in her voice - it didn't matter to Daisy, she had heard it before and knew there was nothing behind it. Chase number seven ended with Daisy throwing the shoe into the main aisle just as her mother caught her. She brought her back, plopped her in the seat beside her and said,

Now, don't you move.

By now many of the other travelers had vacated the area. The oriental teenager - had remained. He would sip his coke and then place it on the seat beside him as he turned pages. A few minutes passed without incident and I returned to my book. Chase number eight occurred when the mother apparently closed her eyes for a moment – dozed off, and the wandering Daisy took the unattended soft drink and made off with it. As she attempted to escape, she tripped and fell, spilling the contents, mostly on the floor, some on herself, and some on the shoes and pants of a business man who had remained in the area.

The mother wiped off Daisy, apologized to the businessman and tried to give the oriental boy enough money to replace the soft drink. The boy, who apparently spoke little English, was incredulous, having never, I'm sure, witnessed such behavior in his life.

Chase number nine was when Daisy ran under the restraining ropes and down the enplaning and deplaning ramp.

Eventually our plane arrived and we began to board. I looked for Daisy and her mother and spotted them being seated in the area of my seat. I thought, *surely God wouldn't do that to me,* a two hour flight from Dallas to Atlanta sitting next to Daisy would be enough provocation to wait for a later flight.

I was right,
God didn't do that to me,
I was two rows behind them.

Can't Wait till Friday

ONE OF THE MOST CHERISHED promises of the Christian life is peace. Although it is promised by Jesus and desired by all – it is actually realized by few. Most of us probably fit into the, *weary and heavy-laden* category, more realistically.

That weariness is the result of societal pressure to accept as a *normal* lifestyle, the concept of *success.* Success is defined as; having something **first**; having **more** of something; or having what others **want.** Well meaning parents begin instilling the success syndrome into their babies. They are very concerned that **their** babies walk, talk, be potty trained **before** anyone else's. Their children must learn to read, write, do calculus and operate a home computer before they go to school. We convince ourselves that it is for *their* good, when actually it may simply be *bragging rights* for us and indoctrination for them, and they haven't reached that first level of intense competition with their rivals – called

kindergarten.

The game becomes even more serious as competition becomes intense for grades, girls, starting positions, student council, class president, etc. Society imposes severe penalties on those who do not compete or are not successful – you have to sit on the sidelines with all of the other losers and misfits. The great misfortune is that many parents not only believe their children are misfits and losers – they tell them that by their words and actions – trying to motivate them to greater effort in the life and death game of–

beating the others.

The pressure of living under the *One Minute Manager* syndrome mounts and anxiety and weariness result. We try to make Friday come more quickly because somehow Friday means peace – a respite from the pressure to manage our minutes. So we wish away the present. We *can't wait* till they're out of diapers, till they go to school, till they learn to drive, till they graduate – till they leave home – till they come back home – till they get married, till our wives get better jobs – till the house is paid for – till we retire – till summer comes – till fall is here – till football season – till football season is over

(is football season **ever** over?)

This *can't wait* concept is based upon an evolutionary view of man. If all we're going to get, ie; happiness, satisfaction, experience – is what we get between the narrow parameters of birth and death – if *life* – really is a ticking clock – sand running between our fingers – then it is right and logical that we should sleep as little as possible – run as fast as we can as long as we can – stimulate our emotions by every available means, have sex as often as possible with whomever is closest – eat as much as possible as often possible – listen to hysterical music – make money by whatever means are available and not be intimidated by morality, integrity, people's feelings, or possible future disasters.

If however, we really believe that sitting at the Lord's feet and listening to His Words is a better choice than running around the kitchen fixing dinner to impress the company – if life has just begun – then all of that is hogwash. There is plenty of time to sleep – to dream – to visit and sing – to play checkers – to fish – to watch the kids grow up – to eat watermelon and read – to watch the moon come out from behind the clouds and to watch the river run by and wonder where it came from – and where it goes. There is plenty of time to get to–

know the Lord.

Do you want to *know the Lord?* God's rest can be ours, but we will never enjoy it as long as we–

can't wait till Friday.

Storytelling

A CHILD WHO GROWS UP WITH a consciousness of who he is - based upon his understanding of the vital link of transmission, which he forms between two ongoing histories, connecting the past with the future - will live more purposefully, thoughtfully and prayerfully. He will be less selfish and develop a wider consciousness and perspective of life and his place in society.

Much of what we call vandalism - Watts riots, L.A. riots, Detroit riots, etc. - the senseless, wanton destruction of property, which has reached epidemic proportions in our culture, is due to a feeling of disenfranchisement, which is sort of like a broken electrical circuit. It destroys any sense of relationship by breaking down our bridges to the past and the future - even to our present surroundings - leaving us isolated. Life itself is seen as an incident - frozen in time - having no relationship to anyone or anything. To the disenfranchised - even parents - family only relate biologically, creating an ever decreasing sense of familial obligation.

The vandal is the end product of what the evolutionists have been telling us that we all are, sophisticated animals - animals with no vital connecting links. Vandalism is an outburst of self-gratification. It is the actualization of a whim, a display of power which brings a sensual type of pleasure, which is the only justification it needs. If we ask a vandal why he did it - if he is educated enough to be articulate, intelligent enough to understand himself, and honest enough to admit it - he would say that he did it because he wanted to, it was fun, and he enjoyed it.

There is a little vandalism in all of us.

Ecological, societal and moral insensitivity is created by the same type of isolation. It is the inevitable outgrowth of humanism. People see no relationship between themselves and their environment -

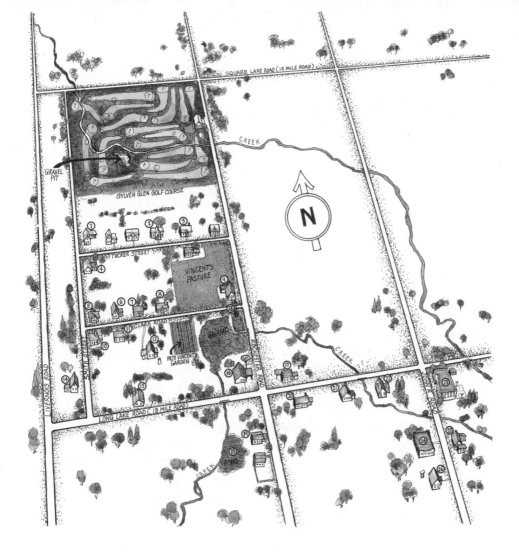

1. ELMER RUSSELL'S HOUSE
2. PETERSON'S HOUSE
3. SPIKE BROWN'S HOUSE
4. CUMBER'S HOUSE
5. SMITH'S HOUSE
6. BUSSEY'S HOUSE
7. PORTER'S HOUSE
8. VINCENT'S HOUSE
9. DICK LAWRENCE'S HOUSE
10. MACFARLAND'S HOUSE
11. MURDOCK'S HOUSE
12. MY HOUSE
13. SALT WATER SWIMMING POOL

14. ERNIE WATSON'S HOUSE
15. OLD MAN TEMAN'S HOUSE
16. MARSHALL BRUDER'S STANDARD OIL STATION
17. BJORNSTEAD'S HOUSE
18. SUDEMEISTER'S POND
19. SUDEMEISTER'S FARM
20. BEAMER'S HOUSE
21. FANNINGSDORF'S HOUSE
22. MOROSO'S HOUSE
23. COLERAIN SCHOOL HOUSE
24. HETHER'S GROCERY STORE
25. CHESNEY'S HOUSE
26. ABERNATHY'S HOUSE

except as it can be manipulated to their gratification – so the extinction of whales, or eagles, the loss of wetlands, the mutilation of rain forests, the threat to the ozone layer, the fouling of rivers, acid rain, and air pollution, are simply minor aggravations to be suffered as we satiate our passion for greater self indulgence. Disasters such as nuclear waste and oil spills are simply vandalism on a large scale by adults who perpetrate the conditions which cause them for the very same reasons that junior high school boys break into school buildings and throw paint on the walls and smash up the furniture. Their isolated view of themselves gives them no sense of gratitude for the past, or indebtedness to the future which would have helped them to transcend the wanton pursuit of momentary pleasures.

When Napoleon's soldiers were in Egypt, they amused themselves by firing their cannons at the Sphinx. They laughed when they succeeded in breaking off its nose. When we ask how they could do such an immoral thing – did they have no sense of the great violation to history – both past and future – that they were committing – the answer is no, they did not! They were behaving exactly like the women who abort their babies and the parasites who assist them. Rape, greed, pornography, homosexuality, abortion and addiction are all prehistoric, animalistic expressions which satisfy whims – with no moral sensitivity – regard for relationships – or consequences. They are self destructive acts of barbarism which temporarily satiate a driving erotic impulse. They are the perfectly predictable conclusions to the evolutionary, humanistic, manipulative culture we have adopted, which has swept all traditional moral foundations away and replaced them with **nothing**.

We must retrace our steps. There is nothing to sustain us in our present direction – we must **go back**. We must rebuild family consciousness. I mean not only the immediate family of parents and children, but the extended family of grandparents, aunts, uncles, and cousins, and ultimately –

the human family.

We can find no better place to start our rebuilding – no better model – than that which is given to us by God in the Old Testament as He laid down the principles which governed the nation of Israel. Those principles led to the founding of the Jewish nation – a nation which has existed for nearly four thousand years because it was not founded on geography, politics or philosophy – it was founded on the divine principle of the family. In spite of their sins – in spite of their stubbornness, disobedience, pride and greed – the Jews have retained their identity because of their fidelity to the principle of maintaining family identity. The vehicle they have utilized most consistently is that of historical perspective, achieved commonly through storytelling. The Jews didn't invent storytelling, they copied it from God. The first five books of the Bible – in fact the Bible itself is a compilation of stories – which all blend into one story and every human being who hears that story can find his place in it.

Storytelling is vital to family success. By success I only mean family consciousness. In a society of fragmented families, far too many children grow to physical maturity with no sense of belonging, or investment in anything which is larger than themselves. This, of course, leads to family breakdown and divorce. Storytelling is a way of teaching and preserving family traditions which allow children to see themselves as part of and vital to an ongoing history. It gives them a definite connection to the past and obligates them to the future. Their whole concept of self-worth rests upon this   identification.

I heard this story told by Fred Craddock, an instructor at the Candler School of Religion at Emory University. He was repeating it as he had heard or read it, by Scott Momaday, a Kiowa Indian, writer and literature professor at Southern California University.

Momaday says that when he was a small boy living in a Kiowa Village, his father waked him unexpectedly very early one morning. He told him to get up and get dressed. He led him by the hand, very sleepily, to the house of an old squaw. He left him there and promised to return that evening. This process was repeated over an extended period of time.

All day this ancient squaw of the Kiowa nation told him stories – sang him the songs of the Kiowa. She explained the rituals and the history of the Kiowa – how they began in a hollow log on the Yellowstone River – how they migrated westward. She told of wars with other tribes – of blizzards, cold, famine. She told him of great chiefs, heroic deeds, of buffalo hunts. She told of the coming of the white man – the clash and the war – of moving north, of moving – always moving, Kansas – Nebraska – diminishing numbers, desperation – finally, Fort Sill, Oklahoma, the surrender, the reservation, confinement, despair and the determination to survive.

Finally, the time of his education was over. Momaday says, *I left her house a Kiowa, I knew what it meant to be a Kiowa. I knew who I was and who my people were, and I knew that I would always be a Kiowa.*

People who have that type of identity are not apt to go around senselessly smashing up the things which give them that identity.

They are not apt to abort the future to satisfy or gratify the totally selfish desires of the moment.

All stories have a point. It may simply be entertainment or it may be a moral lesson. For thousands of years stories were the measure of truth and they still can be used effectively in that way. Stories place truth in perspective. They give truth flavor by attaching names, faces, and geographical locations to abstract notions and emotional realities.

I have tried in this next section to give some examples of stories I have told my children about my childhood and the lessons that I specifically tried to illustrate. Children quickly and easily forget moralistic and practical instruction. It just doesn't seem to stick, but my children have never forgotten these stories and the lessons that were integral to them.

Storytelling is important – vital to family awareness. As you read the stories in this book, I hope you will be inspired to tell stories to your children. If you can't think of stories, read these. You will find your own story here and you can simply use it as a point of departure- .....*that story reminds me of the time when I...*

A Good Memory

OCCASIONALLY, I COME CROSS something in my reading that speaks so forcefully, directly and beautifully to my heart that I realize that I cannot say it better – in this case – I could not say it so well – and so I bring it to you as I found it.

It is from **The Brothers Karamazov,** by Fyodor Dostoyevsky. The setting is this: Alyosha, the speaker, is addressing a group of young boys – probably ten to thirteen years old. They have gathered at, *Ilusha's stone* in memory of their friend Ilusha, who has just died. The stone was a favorite place of his and it was his wish to be buried there. These boys had all been childhood enemies of Ilusha, but in the last days of his life, during his illness, they were reconciled by their teacher, Alyosha, and came to love, not only their former enemy Ilusha –

but each other.

I often beg you to read slowly – let me beg you once again – let these beautiful words wash over your soul. They will bring both cleansing, peace, hope and renewed determination to live a better life.

My dear children, perhaps you won't understand what I am saying to you, because I often speak very unintelligibly, but you'll remember it all the same and will agree with my words sometimes. You must know that there is nothing higher and stronger and more wholesome and good for life in the future than some good memory, especially a memory of childhood, of home. People talk to you a great deal about your education, but some good, sacred memory, preserved from childhood, is perhaps the best education. If a man carries many such memories with him into life, he is safe to the end of his days, and if one has only one good memory left in one's heart, even that may sometime be the means of saving us. Perhaps we may even grow wicked later on, may be unable to refrain from a bad action, may laugh at men's tears and at those people who say as Kolya did just now, "I want to suffer for all men," and may even jeer spitefully at such people. But however bad we may become - which God forbid - yet, when we recall how we buried Ilusha, how we loved him in his last days, and how we have been talking like friends all together, at this stone, the cruelest and most mocking of us - if we do become so - will not dare to laugh inwardly at having been kind and good at this moment! What's more, perhaps, that one memory may keep him from great evil and he will reflect and say, "Yes, I was good and brave and honest then." Let him laugh to himself, that's no matter, a man often laughs at what's good and kind, that's only from thoughtlessness. But I assure you, boys, that as he laughs he will say at once in his heart, "No, I do wrong to laugh, for that's not a thing to laugh at."

Parents have no greater obligation than to create wholesome memories for their children. One of the great purposes for my writing this book is my absolute faith in the sustaining power of memories – especially those that are centered in our understanding of the role of God's providence in our lives.

Where Does the Stuff Go?

MOST OF THE FIRST TEN YEARS of my life were lived in about a square mile. The square mile was bounded by Eighteen Mile Road to the south, Nineteen Mile Road to the north, Rochester road to the east and Livernois Road to the west. I lived very close to the corner of Eighteen Mile Road and Rochester Road, on Clark Road.

To go to school, I walked down Clark Road. (I say *down* because Clark Road sloped uphill from Rochester Road to my house.) Anyway, I walked down Clark Road to Rochester Road, turned south about three hundred yards to Eighteen Mile Road, turned east about one mile to John R. and there it was, Colerain School, three rooms, eight grades, the finest minds of the century being honed to a razor sharp edge – well –

perhaps something slightly less than that.

Walking back and forth to school was a much anticipated daily event. In fact, school itself was anticlimactic. Few days passed without incident and I looked forward to this part of every day, which was an education in itself.

The three hundred yards between Rochester Road and Eighteen Mile Road were particularly gratifying because of the swamp. Rochester Road was the east boundary of the swamp and the edge of the road was lined with cattails and marsh grass. Of course swamp creatures collected there, especially during the dry season – snakes, turtles, crayfish, muskrats, frogs and leeches. On the way to school, my friends and I were always poking around, pulling the reeds apart, prying into every opening, looking for something to catch – or throw rocks at.

About half-way between Clark Road and Eighteen Mile Road was a very large culvert which ran under Rochester Road and drained off the excess water from the swamp. During hard rains, it would be half filled with rushing water, but most of the time it contained only eight or ten inches. The culvert must have been four or five feet in diameter and we walked through it and played in it often. When cars and trucks passed over us, it trembled and echoed, which was deliciously exciting.

On our way to school one morning in late spring – after several days of very heavy rainfall – we were astounded by the fact that the water in the swamp was almost level with Rochester Road – the culvert was totally submerged – but where it normally could be seen, there was now a gigantic whirlpool! It was fascinating. We stood there in unbelief. We had never seen such a thing. We began to throw things into it, sticks, and other debris which had washed up to the edge of the water. Round and round they went – ever increasing in speed, narrowing the circle, drawn inevitably into that central vortex which consumed them and took them from sight.

One of the boys, Freddie Petersen I think, caught a small frog and threw it in. We watched in dumb amazement as the frog struggled frantically to break out of the sucking grip of the whirlpool, but he didn't have a chance. He made some headway at first, but he grew tired – finally, exhausted, he succumbed and he too

disappeared from sight.

It **never occurred** to any of us that the whirlpool was caused by the culvert. You must understand that. We couldn't see it and we did not connect the two things. It was a great mystery – *Where does the stuff go?* – we asked ourselves – *into what horrible, bottomless pit did it ultimately come to spend a dark eternity?*

The whirlpool bothered me all day. I couldn't get it out of my mind. I sat in school thinking about and envisioning it. *Where does the stuff go?* I wondered. I don't know when or how it occurred to me. I believe that somehow in thinking about the whirlpool I created a visual image of the area and in that image I saw the whole scene – like from a helicopter, and in the larger picture I could see the other side of Rochester Road, and the culvert opening, and the creek which was formed by the swamp water. Of course, I thought – the stuff doesn't go **down** at all – it comes out on the other side! – the side we never walk on! I was so happy – so excited I couldn't wait to test my theory on the way home.

I did it very dramatically. I found a piece of wood and carried it with me. I waited until we got to the whirlpool, got everybody's attention and threw it in – when it finally disappeared, I shouted *Come on,* and ran across the road – sure enough – there it came – surging out at an amazing speed. What a victory – they were astounded at my sagacity.

What made me think of the whirlpool after all these years, was thinking about death – what a mystery it is – all life is inevitably drawn in ever increasing speed toward that all consuming, spinning, whirling, central vortex which sucks and pulls at us. We, like the frog, struggle frantically for awhile, when we are young, strong, and feel invincible, but the whirlpool always wins – and that's not so bad except we wonder where we go when we plunge into that tunnel where all is darkness and turbulence and unknown. *Where does the stuff go?* We are frightened and although weary,

we renew the struggle.

I wonder if the mystery of death is not created by the same problem my friends and I had. We simply don't see the whole picture. If we could, we would see the other end of the culvert and realize that–

the stuff comes out on the other side.

I really wanted to jump into that whirlpool and swim through – I wasn't afraid. I knew I could do it because I understood the principle of the whirlpool – that what goes in has to come out – that is the law of whirlpools, they are created by the other end – If you block up the exit end of the culvert – you destroy the whirlpool. Life and death are like that – death is not a bottomless pit – it's like the culvert and every culvert has another opening, which is life. If there wasn't an outlet – there couldn't be an inlet. If death did not lead to life – there would be no death, or life either.

And that's what the bible is for – it's to help us see the *whole picture* so that we don't wander around in a fog wondering what life and death are all about. And that's why christians shouldn't have any fear of death –

because they understand
the principle of life.

Love Your Enemies

MY FIRST SCHOOL WAS CALLED Colerain. I have no idea how it got that name. I guess it must not have been too important because no one ever explained it to us. It had three rooms and it stood at the corner of Eighteen Mile Road and John R. in Troy, Michigan. We had three teachers; Miss Smokey, Miss MacDonald, and Miss Rinault. There was no office, no library, no principal, no gym, no cafeteria, and no nonsense. Miss Smokey was my teacher, she was beautiful, and I loved her. Russell Fanningsdorf came there in February, 1944.

His mother marched him into our classroom, completely unannounced one very cold, overcast morning and placed him before Miss Smokey. She was a portly, red-faced woman, dressed in an ankle length nondescript dress, a huge, thick, black sweater and a babushka. You don't know the word babushka? My goodness, what do they teach in school these days? A babushka is like a headscarf that ties under your chin. She would have made a classic portrait of a seventeenth century peasant woman. She spoke almost no English. I understood only the word *school* and the name *Russell.*

Our school was populated mainly by lower middle class students who consequently dressed very modestly. By comparison, Russell was dressed in rags - and peculiar rags at that.

Russell didn't want to stay. He was obviously terrified. He cried and clung tenaciously to his mother. After communicating her desire to place Russell in our school, she turned and placed both of her hands on Russell's shoulders. I wish I could draw you a picture of that scene. It must have made a heavy impression upon me because I can see them so clearly now; her round, rough, red face, worn by cares, old far before its time; her stubby, calloused, work hardened fingers with the black dirt visible under the broken nails; her short, square body trembling -
she addressed him in German.

I will never know what she said, but Russell stopped crying, squared his shoulders and accepted his fate. Finally, they separated and Russell went to an unoccupied desk in the fourth grade row. He sat all day in absolute silence, never acknowledging our stares or even our presence. He did not go out for recess, or for lunch.

You must understand that it was 1944. Our country was engaged in a bitter conflict with Germany. The Germans were our enemies. Even as children we had learned to hate and there is no discrimination in a child's hatred. Russell was German. He spoke with a German accent.
We hated him.

We would not accept him. He gradually - painfully worked his way into the school routines, but he was a person apart. He was never chosen for a team, he was taunted, heckled, called *Kraut,* and *Nazi* - we would imitate a German salute and say *Heil, Hitler* - he was abused in every way,
and he was alone.

He remained aloof. He did not cry, he did not respond or resist, he would not acknowledge us. He had not a single friend, except Miss Smokey. Her herculean efforts to teach him, to reach him, to help him with his clothes, his speech - and to blast us with her withering looks and speeches for our cruelty, are an everlasting monument to her and to her kind. I thank God for Miss Smokey-
Russell's only friend.

To make matters even worse, the Fanningsdorfs had moved into an old abandoned farmhouse on Eighteen Mile Road, a place so run down and rickety that no one had lived there for years, and there they raised pigs. Russell smelled of pig – and we reminded him of it.

Russell's life with us reached a climax late that spring. As you can easily imagine, he was a poor student. He barely spoke English, he never had paper or pencil, but always suffered the humiliation of having to *borrow* from Miss Smokey. He would not ask of us –
he knew the answer.

One bright, warm, spring day Miss Smokey, in an attempt to rouse the interest of her flagging students, promised an afternoon holiday to our class if everyone scored a hundred on a spelling test. She obviously forgot about Russell. It wasn't a very hard test, and even Russell might have passed it, but he didn't. Whether he was paying us back, or whether he just didn't know, I can't guess. We graded each other's papers and then read the scores out loud. Sure enough, Russell was the only one who missed a word, and we missed our holiday.

Now I come to the hard part. How can I tell you this? What will you think of me? After school, two other boys (Doug Bussey and Tommy Petersen), and I jumped Russell and beat him up. I don't know what good we thought it would do. Even after forty years the ache in my heart is almost unbearable.

Russell never came back to school that year, and I never saw him again until the following fall.

There are two lessons I wish to share with you. First, perhaps some of you who read this, are teachers or plan to teach. I praise God for that – there is no more noble calling on this earth. Our Lord Jesus Christ was called *Teacher.* May God help you to be sensitive to the Russells who come to your schools – your classrooms. In a world of insensitivity may they find in you some understanding – some sympathy – a friend.

Second – Christianity ought to make us better. I am sorry to say that all of the sermons, all of the Sunday School lessons I had heard, and the examples I had seen, did not teach me to *love my enemies.*
Oh, I had been taught the words...
Whatsoever ye would that men should do unto you, do ye even so to them for this is the law and the prophets. Matthew seven and twelve.
I could quote that in my sleep, but the specific **application** was missing. I did not see my attitude toward Russell as being a violation of anything I had been taught. My parents and their friends spoke in hateful terms of the Germans – who they called *Krauts,* Japanese

– who they called *Japs,* Chinese, who they called *Chinks,* Negroes, who they called *Niggers*, and Italians, who they called *Dagos* or *Wops.*

It is no wonder my actions bothered me so little.

Remember, that if there is an inconsistency between your actions and your teaching – a child will nearly always copy your behavior.

Remember also that if our Christianity does not make us better in practical situations it is useless to us.

God calls us to love our enemies –
it's no trouble to love your friends.

Marks

I WAS LOOKING AT MY HANDS this morning and I noticed a small blue dot in the palm of my left one. Hands are amazing things, you know. It is interesting to me that most of my scars are on my left hand – it's because my left hand is nearly always holding the object my right hand is aiming at. I hold the hammer, the knife, the saw, or the screwdriver in my right hand, and I **operate** on whatever the left hand is holding. The scars are the result of missed communication between my hands. But, the blue dot isn't.

It came from another source.

I have had the blue dot for nearly half a century. It was put there by a boy named Donny Hether (pronounced Hee'-ther). He sat right in front of me in the fourth grade. We weren't friends, but then we certainly weren't enemies either. His folks owned a small grocery store right down John R. road, not far from school. I realize that folks don't patronize small, owner operated grocery stores anymore, but back then they did, and the Hethers were considered, *folks with money.* That sort of placed him in a higher category than the rest of us.

Donny had nice clothes and got his hair cut pretty often by a real barber. He also had this stuff on his hair that made it look slick and it smelled real sweet. Kids today would laugh at it, but then it was considered hot stuff. Donny would have been better off not to go to the barber's quite so often, because he had pretty big ears and those close-cropped haircuts made them stand out.

Well, I was real bored in school one day, which happened altogether too often and led to most of my difficulties. The teacher was working with the fifth graders on some problem about the Russians getting half of Germany at the end of World War II, and I wasn't too interested - apparently neither was our government. Anyway, I got to noticing Donny's right earlobe. It was because his head was right in front of my face, and from the rear the most outstanding feature of his head was his ears, and the most outstanding thing about his ears was his earlobes. Earlobes are a wonder - an absolute marvel. You know, they just sort of hang down there beside your head, kinda' soft and floppy and completely useless. I didn't know then that your earlobes are inherited, and that some folks' earlobes are closely attached to their heads, and other folks have earlobes which aren't -

Donny's weren't attached!

I could feel a powerful temptation sweeping over me to just reach up and flick his right earlobe and watch it jiggle. I fought it down several times because I really didn't have a reason - besides meanness - and I also had some notion that he might be sort of surprised and perhaps not take it too friendly. Well, it got the best of me. I got my index finger locked real good behind my thumb and I squeezed down until it fairly exploded. I thumped that earlobe and it flapped like a clothesline sheet in a twenty mile an hour wind.

Donny never yelped, nor moved. It was the most remarkable display of nerves and self-discipline I ever saw. About two minutes later, he turned around. I had my left hand laying open - palm up on my desk - and he had this brand new, freshly sharpened yellow pencil - and he stuck it right in the palm of my hand. The lead broke off and stayed there. He turned around and went right back to his work.

I never bothered Donny much after that.

The mark is still there, and I suspect that it's the only reason I remember Donny Hether. I have some other marks - some visible - some you can't see. They were put there by folks who touched my life in one way or another. I wonder how many folks are wandering around this earth with my marks on them? And-

I wonder what kind of marks they are?

God put a mark on Cain, the Bible says, and you could see it. It puzzles me what it might have been. John tells us in Revelation that the redeemed have God's name written on their foreheads. I can't

see it in the mirror, but I sure hope I have it. I guess we all leave marks of one kind or another on folks every day. Maybe we ought to be more cautious because sometimes-

even after fifty years,
that's how we're remembered.

"And the Life Was the Light of Men"

WHEN I WAS NINE THEY BEGAN the process of draining the swamp below our house. I didn't know that was what they were doing, so when the big drainage ditch was dug and the pipe laid in it, I was only fascinated by the size of the machinery and the excitement of the event. If I had known their intent, I'm sure I would have sabotaged the operation. I loved the swamp. Every day I was there, watching and getting in the way as the crew of men used a giant back-hoe to dig the trench.

When they left, only the mounded ribbon of fresh dirt which covered the pipe remained as evidence of their passing. A most peculiar thing happened, which has to do with the best laid plans of mice and men, I suppose. Their theory was to drain the swamp into a creek which ran about three or four hundred yards away. There was a rise in the ground, on top of which was the road to our house, which separated the north end of the swamp from the creek. Not long after they finished the drainpipe, we had several days of heavy rainfall, the creek flooded, the water ran from the creek, through the drain pipe and poured into the swamp. Where it emptied into the swamp, the velocity of the rushing water dug out a huge hole which later formed a large pool.

Swamp life migrated to this pool. Fish, leeches, turtles, muskrats, frogs and even ducks and geese were found there in abundance. It became a favorite place. I often found myself in the pool chasing something. Inevitably, I was drawn to the mouth of the drain pipe. It ran reasonably straight and you could actually see through it -

a tiny white speck of light,
which winked and beckoned to me.

I entered the pipe on several occasions, but it was a very tight fit and backing up was almost impossible, so after a few feet I always squirmed back out.

It was inevitable that I must try it.

One day my boyfriend, James MacFarland, and I had been chasing a large turtle in the pond, but it eluded us by going into the drain pipe which was just at water level. I went into the pipe to get the turtle, determined that it was not going to escape from me that easily. James followed me. I had gone quite a ways, intent upon the turtle, before I realized that he was there, and I had come much farther in than ever before. James was slightly larger than I and when I stopped, he bumped into me, I had a sinking feeling. He could not back up. *Did you get him?* he yelled. The muffled echo in those close quarters scared us. *No,* I whispered, *I guess he got away.* When James tried to back up he realized what a predicament we were in and he panicked. I wasn't exactly happy, but I could see the light and he couldn't. Mustering my most cheerful, reassuring voice I said,

Let's just crawl all the way through.

It took us about an hour, I think. In places the pipe was low, and collected water lay within four or five inches of the top. Nasty, smelly, mucky water, filled with leeches, which had been there since the last rain. With heads pushing hard against the top, noses tilted up high as possible, we crawled on. We bloodied our knees and toes on the rough concrete and the tops of our heads were scraped clean of either hair or skin as we attempted to keep water out of our noses, and of course, the turtle swam and crawled constantly before us, completely oblivious to the circumstances. When we finally fell out the other end into the sunlight and fresh water of the creek-

I was a very grateful young lad.

Looking back, I reflect on what kept me going. Although I had my fearful moments, I can honestly say that I kept James going and even enjoyed the adventurous feeling I had. He knew we were going to die, that we would never be found, and he cried the whole way and constantly despaired. For the whole time, the entire distance, he never turned loose of my ankle. Sometimes I look at my ankle even now, my left one to be exact, and I imagine that I can see the imprint of his desperately clutching fingers and the cuts he made with his fingernails. I whispered to him constantly of my confidence, my hope. *Not far now, James, almost there, James, we're going to make it, James, don't worry, James.*

Do you know what the difference was? Have you guessed my secret? Do you think I was the braver? The more determined? No – no, a thousand times NO! The difference was that I could see the light! I could see the light! What a marvelous spiritual application that has! We live in a world of darkness, of dreary hopeless places which constantly threaten to suffocate us. There are voices which call us to quit, to see that it's hopeless – but there is the light – the light which beckons us and invites us – the sweet light of hope and promise which is Jesus Himself. And the Light says–

Not far now, John,
Almost there, John,
Just a little more,
You're going to make it,
Don't lose heart, John,
I'm with you, John.

Fear

IT WAS MARCH 31, 1944 OR 1945. I remember the date because it was my birthday. Either my birthday fell on a Saturday that year, or it was the Saturday after when this event took place. Traditionally, I always took my first swim of the year on my birthday. It wasn't a very old tradition because I wasn't very old, but I had done it for two or three years in a row

which to a child is an old tradition.

Even in years when spring came early, it was a real test of fortitude in Michigan. This year spring was very late. The ice had only been gone for a week or so, and the deep, clear, blue-green spring water which filled the abandoned gravel pit was only slightly above freezing. It was a gray, overcast, windy, March day. We stood on the bank in our birthday suits deliberating. We had huge chill bumps standing out all over our bodies and we hadn't even gotten wet yet. We looked at each other, Tommy, Freddie, James and I, hoping that somebody would say, *I'm going home, this is stupid,* but we were just boys and we still believed that displaying strength was greater than showing wisdom.

It's your birthday, James stated, *you should go in first,* to which Tommy and Freddie both immediately assented. *You guys are just chicken,* I retorted, *but I'm going to go.* There was nothing else but to do it, and so I did. Tommy and Freddie were right behind me but James stayed. James was the intellectual in our group. It wasn't far, thirty yards maybe, to our destination, which was an island in the gravel pit, but I would have never made it. I simply grew so numb with cold that I had no control over my arms and legs. Freddie was two years older than I - much stronger and a better swimmer - he grabbed me and helped me to the shore. It was not a case of maybe, it simply was a fact that I would have drowned without him.

Now I was faced with a terrible dilemma. I was on the island, the cold wind on my wet, naked body was unbearable and there was only one way back - the same way that I got there - swimming. James said he would go and get my dad, but it didn't take long to decide that drowning was by far the better of those two evils. I was not long making up my mind. I dove in and thrashed my way blindly to shore like a demon was after me. I even outdistanced Freddie. I was shocked, when my outstretched hands began grabbing gravel, and I guess I was six feet up the bank before I quit trying to swim. I dressed as quickly as possible and headed for home.

A person rarely performs at his capacity unless there is appropriate motivation. I have been motivated by anger, by reason and by love. In this case, I was motivated by fear, fear of discovery, fear of dying, and fear of what that meant. Let there be no doubt that God not only knows that, but has consistently used it to produce the desired results in His children. Any parent who mistakenly refrains from motivating their children through this medium severely handicaps their potential for successful child rearing.

Appropriate use of fear is a valuable tool in child rearing. The divine stamp of approval has been placed upon it.

Let me caution you to think about the word *appropriate* - fear motivation must never be an excuse for bullying or cruelty. God is a God of balance - of propriety, and He would have us to imitate His wisdom.

Summer of Forty Five
the Other Side of Fear

I WAS EIGHT THAT SUMMER, so were James, Tommy, and Doug. It was another turning point in my life, although I didn't know anything about turning points, and I certainly didn't mean for it to be.

I had much simpler things in mind.

The Salt Water Swimming Pool was right down the hill from our house. Looking back, it seems very strange that there should be a swimming pool near us, because we lived in a very sparsely settled, rural area. How it got there, or why, still puzzles me, but it was there, right on the corner of Clark Road and Rochester Road.

It had two diving boards, one about three feet off the water and one about twelve feet. I watched with envy and admiration as the older boys strode with measured, rhythmic steps to the end, jumped high, pushed down hard and allowed the spring of the boards to propel them high into the air as they dove gracefully into the water. I walked out on the three foot board in 1943, when I was six. I remember the growing fear, the queasiness in my stomach, as I gingerly edged my way to the end. When I looked down, the water was unbelievably far away. I closed my eyes and I jumped, shocked at how soon I hit the water. Before the summer was over I was jumping and diving regularly and fearlessly, and I began to look apprehensively at the twelve foot board.

The next summer, when I was seven, my friends and I made a pact that we would conquer the twelve foot board. I was the first to try it. I walked out slowly, careful to stay in the middle lest I fall off, and I looked down. The distance to the water was beyond belief. I stood long at the end of the board, my friends taunting me, but the dizzying nausea in my stomach made my legs weak and broke my will. I was absolutely frozen with fear, and gently, ever so slowly, I placed one foot behind the other and retreated to the safety of the platform. Several days passed, and all of my friends succeeded, before I tried it again. Once again, by the end of summer it was a regular thing.

There was another board. Not a diving board really and you are going to have to use your imagination to see this – and you must really see it to appreciate it. An iron pipe about four inches in diameter had been sunk into the concrete immediately in front of the platforms which supported the diving boards. It was attached,

for stability, to the platforms at both levels and it rose some ten feet above the twelve foot platform. An iron ladder, about eight inches in width, had been welded to the pipe at the twelve foot level. It had iron rungs so small in diameter that they hurt your feet. At the top of the iron pipe was a socket, into which was placed the flagpole, and attached to the pipe, right at the socket was a small platform, about six inches wide and two feet long. During the summer of forty-five Tommy, Doug, James, and I vowed we would dive from that platform.

I went up the ladder twice, early that summer, to insert the flagpole into its place. Going up was relatively easy because the tendency is to fix your eyes on your destination, and you don't have to look or feel for the rungs, like you do on the way down. Once the flag was in place, I would first look around - amazed at what I could see from my vantage point. Then my eyes would be drawn down - down to the water. That sick, nauseous feeling and the frightening dizziness would come, causing me to cling to the ladder desperately. I would close my eyes - establish my equilibrium, and very slowly begin searching for the next lowest rung, and the next, knowing that I must not open my eyes until I could feel the wooden platform.

Tommy tried it first. It was July. He made it to the top of the ladder, but he had to be pried loose from it by the lifeguard because he wouldn't release his grip. His pleas for help caused all of us to be very sober. Two weeks later James tried it, he did better. He made it to the top of the ladder, but it ended at the flagpole socket, so you had to hold on to the flagpole itself as you climbed the last three rungs and the flagpole wasn't very steady with the wind pulling the flag and bending the pole. Balancing was very tricky. James tried to crawl onto the platform on his hands and knees but it was too small. In the process, he lost his nerve and nearly fell.

August came, the time grew short, the summer of forty-five was almost at an end. Doug moved that summer and we never saw him again, it took some of the spirit out of our resolve. Every day I would stand and look up at the flagpole. The joy of the other boards was greatly diminished and the pool wasn't as much fun.

One morning it rained, but early in the afternoon the sun came out for a short time. I went to the pool alone. I knew what I was going to do. I practiced climbing the ladder. I must have gone up and down twenty times or more. I was determined to conquer my fear of the ladder. Finally I was able to rest at the top, and even to look down without getting sick and dizzy. I made a plan for how to get out on the board, memorized every hand hold and movement. I knew I must do it quickly, I must never hesitate, never consider what could go wrong and once on the board I must dive immediately.

That night I prayed much about it and the next day I did it. I did it just like I had planned. I stepped out on the board, closed my eyes and without hesitation I dove.

It seemed an eternity before I hit the water.

Words will fail me here. The sensation, not just of the rush of air as I fell, nor the incredible shock - jolt, from hitting the water, but of swimming to the edge - climbing out, being surrounded by my friends and then standing there looking at where I had just been, was overwhelming. It was amazing how different that platform looked from the other side. Very few times in my fifty-three years have I experienced that type of completely satisfying exhilaration. I was on the other side of fear, the affirmative side - the side you can only know about if you have the **faith** to pass through it. Those whose **unbelief** causes them to back away on the front side, only know fear as a deterrent - only experience the nausea, the dizziness, the paralyzing, terrifying frustration of defeat.

I have been afraid many times since. I have experienced all of its effects, down to the sweaty palms, but I believe that the summer of forty-five established a precedent for moving through fear. Just as the fear experience builds and increases if we respond negatively, so those who pass through - those who experience the other side of fear - the positive side, are those for whom fear becomes an incentive. Although they experience the symptoms of fear, even those very symptoms become a source of motivation, because they anticipate the other side.

> The summer of forty-five -
> The other side of fear.
> No one can take you through it-
> You must climb the ladder alone-
> And you must climb it by faith.

I Got away with it

MY GUN CASE CONTAINS A WIDE variety of weapons. Some of them are quite expensive and carefully made. There is one there which is neither expensive or well made, but it never fails to attract attention. When people ask, *What's that?* (It is a model 42 Winchester pump twenty-two), I'm sure they notice the solemnity and reverence with which I pick it up. The bluing is completely gone, the stock has been broken in two and is held together with two brass machine screws. The barrel has a swollen place, because it was fired one time with an obstruction in it. My father traded Elmer Russell a 38 caliber pistol for it in 1943. He told me it was to be mine, but he kept it in his room. Sometimes in the late summer evenings, or on Sunday afternoons, he would take it out and we would shoot tin cans.

I don't think he ever specifically told me that I was not to take it out when he was not there, but I guess I knew it. One Saturday, my folks went shopping. They either took my sister or she walked to a girlfriend's house, anyway, I was at home alone. What made me think of the gun was finding a loaded twenty two shell at a sort of local dump, not too far from our house. I put it in my pocket but-
it seemed to burn a hole there.

When I got home, thoughts of that gun completely occupied my mind. I knew better, but I simply could not overcome the urge to get it. One of my predominant thoughts was, *no one will ever know.* Somehow that seemed to be convincing. If they did not know, it couldn't be wrong. I got the gun, loaded it, and began looking for a target. I only had one shell, so I had to be selective. I wanted to shoot a bird but my father's stern warnings about firing it in the air carried too much weight - I had visions of breaking a window two miles away and getting caught. Ultimately I shot a tin can by the chicken coop - it was very unrewarding. An unloaded gun is not much fun, so I hastily put it away.

I don't think my folks ever found out. At least it was never mentioned and I'm sure that means they didn't know. I guess you could say I got away with it, but I didn't. For days - weeks afterward, I lived in mortal fear that my father would somehow discover my disobedience.

Every time I look at that gun I remember.

My father always meant for me to have the gun and to enjoy it. But he wanted me to enjoy it on those terms which were best for

me. The gift had great potential for me if used properly –
according to his instructions.

I haven't changed much, it's just that my Heavenly Fathers' gifts to me have grown much more expensive and have far greater possibilities for my use and fulfillment. I continue to abuse them, to use them indiscriminately and for purposes for which they were not intended. I still think I can, *get away with it,* and that if it is not known, there can be no harm. It is not so. The tragic part is that when I use His gifts contrary to their purpose and His intentions, they become a curse to me, a source of guilt and depression.

God and the Nickel

POP WAS ONLY A NICKEL. In other places they called it, *Coke* or *Soda,* but we always called it *Pop,* and it was only a nickel. It's hard to believe, but unless you understand that, you won't get much out of the story. Nickels were hard to come by – that's why pop was a nickel – something about economics – the law of supply and demand. Anyway, there was this Standard Oil Station on the corner of Eighteen Mile Road and Rochester Road, which was about a half mile from my house. It was owned by a guy named Marshall Bruder, which isn't too important, but it's neat to know if you're into that sort of thing. Well, Marshall Bruder sold candy out of a glass case and he had a red pop machine with *Coca Cola* written in white cursive letters on the side. It was one of those old kind that had real cold water in the bottom and the bottles of pop sat right down in the water – that's what made them cold, in case you're a little slow on the uptake, and that's also what made them so desirable – the pop I mean – you know, you don't ever see adds saying,
Get your room temperature pop right here.

On real hot days in the summer time, I used to go to Marshall Bruder's with Tommy and Freddie Petersen. We used to go to Marshall Bruder's Standard Oil Station because the concrete floors inside were so smooth and cool on our bare feet, and we would open the lid and stick our hands way down deep – as far as we could reach

- in the Coca Cola machine in that ice cold water. It was delicious.
Mrs. Bruder would eventually run us out. Not too quickly - she
wasn't mean or anything. When we left, we'd get a drink out of their
artesian well. The water was cold and sweet. They had this rock wall
all around the well and it formed a sort of pool - very small, but it
was a neat place to play.

I want to get back to the pop machine though. Every time I
opened that lid I would think how neat it would be to say, *Gimme
a pop,* just like my dad - or some other grown ups who came into
Marshall Bruder's. *Gimme a pop,* I used to practice saying that when
I was alone - I'd walk down Clark Road saying, *Gimme a pop* - I'd
walk around the house saying, *Gimme a pop* - My mother would say,
What? and I'd say - *Oh nothin* - I wanted to be able to say it like a
grown up - *Gimme a pop.* They had Coca Cola, but they also had
R.C. Cola, Byerly's Grape and Nesbitt's Orange. That was what I
really wanted. When Mr. Bruder would say, *what kind of pop?* I'd say,
Nesbitt's Orange. But I never had a nickel, neither did Tommy or
Freddie. Things grow in a child's mind - they get out of proportion
and that's what led me to do something unthinkable.

We went to this real small church that met in a Masonic Lodge in
Hazel Park, Michigan. My dad led singing - another guy - Bob
Winegar did too, but my dad was the *real* song leader. Brother Utley
was the preacher. It was a real good church. I liked going to church
there because Brother Utley was a soft spoken, kindly sort of man
who talked to the kids like they were people, and he got the boys
up in front and asked us Bible questions, and taught us to lead singing
and he never yelled or scared me. My dad led singing, which I
already said, but he was a very good song leader and he made me like
to sing because he was obviously enjoying himself.

After communion they took up the collection. It was sort of
confusing to me because when they took up the collection, they
always said it was, *separate and apart,* from the Lord's Supper, but even
a child could see that it wasn't. The money went in these wicker
baskets with green velvet bottoms. The bottoms were soft like that
so you wouldn't be embarrassed when you dropped change in the
basket. I figured that out by myself. When it was all collected, they
put the baskets with the money up front under the communion
table. I don't know if the idea seized me all at once, or if it crept over
me very subtly and slowly. I only know that one Sunday after church,
while everybody was outside visiting, because it was so hot inside,
I went back inside, walked right up to the communion table, and

took a nickel out of the collection plate. I guess I thought that God wouldn't mind losing a lousy nickel for a bottle of pop, I mean - what's a nickel to God. It's very important that you understand that I could have taken anything - a five dollar bill even. But I didn't want

a five dollar bill-
I wanted a nickel,
wanted one so badly,
that I risked
going to hell,
to get it.

Nobody ever knew. I put it in my pocket and the next day when Tommy, Freddie and I went to Marshall Bruder's, I had it with me. But when the time came to say, *Gimme a pop,* I couldn't do it - I mean the words just wouldn't come out and it scared me because I would try to say the words and I couldn't. I tried it the next day, and it was worse, so I put the nickel in a shoe under my bed and I didn't touch it again. But it haunted me. I couldn't get it out of my mind. I couldn't sleep, and when I did I had terrible dreams. God would speak to me, He would say in a very loud voice - *Where is My nickel? - I want My nickel.* He was so real to me - so incredibly, practically real and I realized I had done a terrible thing - committed a sin beyond reckoning - I had stolen money right out of God's very own pocket and-

I was terrified.

I couldn't wait for Sunday to come - I was so anxious to get to church I was in a sweat. I prayed that God would just let me live long enough to put that nickel in the collection tray when it was passed so the nightmare would be over, and I would know that I was forgiven.

Sunday came. When we got to church I couldn't sing, somehow it didn't seem right and I didn't hear anything Brother Utley said. All I could think about was that nickel in my pocket - and here I was, right in God's presence and anything could happen. Brother Utley might stop any moment and say, *we have a thief in our midst,* and every eye would turn toward me, because somehow they would know. They might prove who stole it by casting lots - like they did with Achan - I always figured it was sort of like a game we played called *Odd Man Out,* and I would get the short stick, then I would be stoned to death. My mother had given me a coin to put in the collection tray, but as it came I found it impossible to put the extra nickel in without detection, because we sat up front and there wasn't anything else in the basket.

My plan was foiled.

After church everybody went outside just like the week before. I crept very carefully back in, but this time with much fear and reverence – like a Jew approaching the Ark of The Covenant – I approached the communion table. I was trembling from head to foot – absolutely terror stricken. I prayed a little prayer, bent over, and placed the nickel, very gently, back into the collection tray and ran out of the building as rapidly as I could.

I was so happy, so relieved, so forgiven. No prisoner ever experienced a greater thrill of freedom and forgiveness. God had graciously made it possible for me to come back into His presence. I felt so good that I sang church songs in the back seat of the car on the way home.

Somewhere I lost some of that sense of God's real presence, with the awe and reverence it brought. **Somehow I have grown to believe that God is not concerned with the nickels I steal from Him, and I no longer tremble with fear at His displeasure.** Somehow I have developed an almost casual and relaxed attitude toward the sanctuary – after all, it's **only** brick and mortar – and I do not hasten, anxiously into His presence with cries of penitence, and I have less sense of joy in forgiveness.

> *Restore unto me the joy of your salvation;*
> *Renew my sense of Your divine presence;*
> *Help me to understand my sinfulness,*
> *May I once again rejoice in the cross of Jesus*
> *and may I never again take for granted,*
> *the grace You have bestowed.*
> *May I be so overwhelmed by your faithfulness*
> *That I sing with gladness your praises,*
> *and shout the majesty of your name.*
> *May your presence be so real that*
> *I fall to my knees and cry,*
> *Holy, Holy - Holy is the Lord of Hosts.*

A Christmas Memory

IN 1946 WE HAD CHRISTMAS dinner at Aunt Velma's. I was nine. Aunt Velma was my mother's youngest sister. She was married to my uncle Brett Snoddy - pronounced, *Snow'-dee*. They were always pretty touchy about their last name so I want to make sure I don't offend them - though I haven't seen any of them for thirty years at least.

Aunt Velma had five children - Brett, Jr., Bobby, Sidney, Nancy, and David. David was my age and Nancy was my sister's age. Brett Jr. and Bobby were much older than me.

In 1946 the Snoddys were living in a log house - it had an open ceiling with big log support beams - it was fascinating. Anyway, Brett Jr. and Bobby had been drafted because of the war and I had not seen them in a long time - but now the war was over and they were going to be home for Christmas.

We got there pretty early and we opened presents. Brett Jr. was there when we got there, but Bobby wasn't and I could tell that Aunt Velma was upset about it. I heard her tell my mom that Bobby had called and said he was trying to hitch-hike because he didn't have money for a bus.

The day went by pretty quickly for me - we built a huge and elaborate snowman, complete with a carrot nose, charcoal ears and a top hat and scarf. Then we had a snowball fight, after which we went ice skating on the creek that ran near their house. Aunt Velma postponed dinner as long as she could - but Bobby didn't show. Finally, we sat down to eat without him. Aunt Velma set a place for Bobby and she had put a chair for him at the table. I think it sort of made everybody solemn -

looking at that empty chair.

The Snoddy's weren't religious people and usually they just dove right into whatever was on the table, but today Aunt Velma asked my dad to pray. Her voice was all shaky and choked up and when I looked at her I saw that she was crying - the tears were running down her cheeks and dripping right into her plate. It took her a minute or two to get it out, but she asked my dad to pray that God would take care of her Bobby and send him home.

Everybody got real sad, we all bowed our heads, but my dad didn't get right into his prayer, for some reason, and when he did, it was a lot different from the one he usually prayed - the one I could say by heart. When he finished, it was pretty quiet for awhile – but then we started passing things and eating and talking and everybody sort of got loosened up – like you always do – and we laughed and told stories. Even Aunt Velma joined in.

It was a great dinner.

We were eating dessert when it happened – I mean we had totally forgotten – but He hadn't. One of the boys said, *Somebody just pulled into the driveway.* – then we heard a car door slam and there was a knock on the door. It's funny how you react to things. Nobody got up – we just looked at each other – Aunt Velma was already up – serving dessert – *It's Bobby,* she cried, *God has sent Bobby home, I just know He has.*

Now Velma, don't get your hopes up, said Uncle Brett, *it's probably someone else.* Nobody could beat Aunt Velma to the door. She was determined that it was Bobby – and it was. I don't know what anybody else thought, because we didn't talk about it, but I never doubted for one minute that God had sent Bobby home –

and I still don't doubt it.

I was nine. Sometimes I think those marvelous events were just for me –

> For me to remember
> when I have doubts.
> For me to tell you about,
> when you have doubts.

The Kingdom of Heaven

*The kingdom of heaven is like a merchant
seeking fine pearls, and upon finding one pearl
of great value, he went and sold all that he had,
and bought it.*

MARBLES WAS THE GAME WE played. There was no basket or ball for basketball, no one owned a football, baseball took too much time for recess or lunch hour so we played marbles. We played for keeps. We drew circles about five feet in diameter in the dirt, and everyone contributed a prearranged number of marbles to the *pot*. The idea was to knock them across the line of the circle. Any marble that rolled out belonged to the *shooter*. There were rules against *hunching, eyedroppers* and *throwing*.

There were three basic kinds of marbles – *aggies, steelies, and peries.* Everybody had a favorite shooter, a special marble prized above all the others. Mine was a perfect *peri*. I do not know the derivation of the word and I spelled it *by ear,* but we used it to signify a marble which was above average in size, absolutely clear, and perfectly round. There were only two or three in the entire school, so it was quite a prize.

My teacher, Miss Smokey, allowed marbles on the playground and marbles in the pockets, but any marble in the school building which became *visible* was hers. She collected hundreds, during the course of the year. A boy, who had suffered severe losses to my *peri,* persuaded me to show it to him in the boy's bathroom. When I produced it, he slapped it out of my hand and ran to Miss Smokey. She took it. I mourned the loss of my shooter like a lost friend.

Since Miss Smokey had no use for marbles, she devised a fascinating way of giving them back. Late in the spring she would take her hoard and place them in a box on top of her desk. Then she had the boys line up behind the desk, when she tipped over the box we would scramble after them.

I got in a very advantageous position, having remembered where all the marbles went the previous year, and consequently seized upward of a hundred marbles – but not the one I wanted. It was found by a third grader. I offered him a nickel, but he declined. I offered to bust his head for him but he declined that offer also, and since he had an eighth grade brother, I didn't push the issue. We finally settled – the hundred marbles for my peri.

It wasn't hard, I mean, I wasn't even reluctant. I was so glad to get my shooter back, that I thought it was the greatest trade I ever made. All those other marbles were absolutely useless. I carried my shooter home, stopping along the way to take it out of my pocket, and hold it up to the sunlight to admire its flawless perfection–

and I was happy.

I wish I could say I still have that marble. Like kites, toy trucks and tricycles, age replaced the fervor and marbles no longer occupied my thoughts. The marble passed quietly out of my life. I have my

memories, and I remember how totally happy I was - absolutely satisfied, with my trade. Today, I know how that pearl merchant felt, and I know that–
the *kingdom of heaven* is my pearl of great price.

Maybe the reason I am often unhappy in my quest for that great pearl is that I see what I'm trading as having value, and I'm reluctant to give up so much of *certain* value for something of *uncertain* value.

Edith

MY FATHER BOUGHT THE HUGE, old, two-story house at 723 Gardenia from a man named A.N. Allen. I know because I've still got an ancient, gold pocket watch of his that has his initials stamped on it. We always called him, *old man Allen*. When we bought the house, the old man asked if he could stay a *few days* until he found another place to live, and my dad agreed. He slept on an old sofa that was in the dining room.

I was eleven.

We soon discovered that he was a drunk, a pitiful, sad old man who was so enslaved that he had lost his job, his family, his friends, and his respect. The few days he wanted to stay with us turned into a nightmare of weeks. He wandered in at every hour of the night, hopelessly drunk, staggering, falling over furniture, cursing, finally collapsing fully clothed on his urine soaked couch, to sleep fitfully until his craving took him once again in search of the only cure to his misery that he knew. My father couldn't bring himself to turn him out into the street. He tried to reason and pray with him,

but it did no good.

He had been married. His wife's name was Edith. She was dead now. The neighbors told us that during her last years she had been an invalid, confined to the house and mostly to bed. Their children had married and moved far away, so the old man was solely responsible for her care. She lay for days with no food, no medical attention, unable to get to the bathroom, until the neighbors heard her cries and came to her assistance.

He was on a binge.

Time after time it happened. I do not doubt that he loved her, or had loved her. I do not doubt that he **wanted** to do better - that he determined often that he **would** do better, but he was so completely in the grip of that demon which tormented, instructed, and directed his every waking moment, that he forgot her. She lay alone, uncared for, and one day - in that very condition - she died.

It haunted him. It drove its way even into the confused, desolate, surrealistic dreams of his drunken stupors. His tortured, delirious voice would cry out in agony, reverberating through the house. It will always ring in my ears. It was never more than one word, *Edith,* he would wail in his despair, *E-dith! E--dith!* His voice would rise higher and higher until it shattered - cracked and broke, subsiding quickly into silence. But Edith was beyond his voice, beyond his ability to forget or neglect, or to help or hurt ever again. I laid in my bed and shuddered with the desolation, wretchedness and despair which tormented him.

I don't know what happened to him. My father was forced to make him leave finally, and I guess he crawled off into whatever long forgotten corner that his kind always crawl to, and he died. And no one cared, and no T.V. commercials were made about *gusto,* or *good times,* or *good friends* - or even worse - *know when to say when.*

I wondered when he was young and handsome, surrounded by friends and admirers, how it started? Who encouraged him to drink the first one, or the second? At every turn of the road where his path might have taken a new direction, which of Satan's cohorts urged his feet back into the rut which grew constantly deeper and whose ultimate destination was predetermined. When his wife pleaded, when his children begged, when his friends warned-
what was the voice he obeyed?

How is it possible to be moderate, tolerant, understanding toward the sale of alcohol; the blatant advertising lies, the deliberate, premeditated deceit of an industry which peddles its wares of destruction and hopelessness in the name of good times, good friends, home, family, community pride, the great outdoors, and eternal happiness, with the big question being-
great taste or less filling?

Both my father and God pointedly used this event to clarify in my mind what the dangers of alcohol are. Old man Allen made such a vivid impression on me that when I was older and the opportunity and the temptation came to initiate the drinking habit-
I shrunk from it in horror.

Sports
And the Home of the Brave

SPORTS ARE IMPORTANT. I could wish that they were not so important as they have become, but there is no doubt that they impact family life dramatically. Even in my rural community of Troy, Michigan, fifty years ago sports were important. At every church picnic there was a hotly contested all-afternoon softball game. At my little three room school I played baseball and marbles. In the winters we had ice skating and sledding - both of which were highly competitive, especially ice skating. We played tag, red rover - red rover, crack the whip, and I developed my second athletic passion, ice hockey - baseball was my first. Later, when we moved to town, it was football, then basketball, golf and tennis. I learned, all too soon, the exhilaration of competition and my life was totally dominated for years with concepts of-

winning and losing.

There have been many positive experiences for me in sports, many memorable occasions, but I caution you that the overall impact has probably been negative. My life has been terribly unbalanced by athletics and I have wandered farther from the Kingdom of God because of sports than I have from any other single facet of my life, save one.

As parents, you will make lasting impressions on your children in this area, both as spectators, supporters, and participants. Athletic parents not only display their true natures when they play, but when they watch and as they drive home. Lectures on sportsmanship, correct attitudes, being a good loser and maintaining balance relative to outcomes, the judges' decisions, and luck aren't really worth much if your conduct belies your words.

I freely confess to you that in no area have I failed my children and myself to a greater degree than in this one. There are many stories that I could write about my actions as a player and as a coach, with my children in the audience or even participating with me, that have left a lasting impression on them which is totally out of harmony with what they have heard me teach - all of their lives.

To our children, we are always parents - at home, at work, on the athletic field, at church, or driving down the highway. Again, I remind you that consistency between behavior and teaching is what remains. It's how you react under pressure that really counts and it's almost impossible to plan for those moments because they come so unexpectedly. I think the most outstanding thing about my parent's attitude toward my athletic endeavors was in their almost total neutrality. I do not remember my mother ever attending an athletic contest I was involved in, except one junior high baseball game. Sports, to my mother were not something to waste a great deal of time on - time that could better be spent stocking the grocery shelves at the B & C Market or anyplace else I could find a job.

My father was not quite as negative and he came to several of my games and sometimes even to practice - especially football. He never got involved though, he wasn't a booster club member or anything. I honestly can't remember him saying anything, pro or con except a very quiet, *that was a good game* - or, *I'm sorry you lost*. The only exception to that was my involvement in ice hockey, which is a story of its own that I will write down one day.

Looking back, I think their attitude was a healthy one. If they had been rabid fans, real cheerleaders who allowed their lives and schedules to be dominated by physicals, uniform fittings, practice schedules, games and booster club activities, I believe it would have made it even worse for me. As it was - the little balance I maintained was probably due to the very casual, off-handed attitude they took. If my games fit into their schedule fine, if not, I was on my own.

I hope you will gain a perspective on athletics that perhaps you haven't had before.

I hope you will laugh,
and cry,
and think -
and be better.

Cross Country

MY SON LINCOLN RAN CROSS country in high school. He wasn't a spectacular runner, although he was a determined one. I think he ran his best in nearly every race - it was never good enough to win but I was pleased with his effort and his dedication and I attended every meet that I could.

There was another boy on the team, a close friend of Lincoln's who was a gifted runner. I will call him Tim. He had red hair and a great smile and I liked him. His father was a very successful business man in town who dressed very stylishly and drove flashy cars. In a town like ours you couldn't help but notice things like that.

Most cross country races involved more than two schools and the one I want to tell you about was no exception. I don't remember how many schools were involved, I do remember that there was a much larger turn out than normal because everybody was interested in the match up between Tim and another state class athlete, a Mexican American boy from Lake Havasu.

I still remember the marked contrast between the two boys. Tim - very tall and slender, very fair, red headed, with long, smooth, powerful strides and the Mexican American boy, dark skinned, dark haired, short, stocky, with quick almost jerky strides.

Tim's dad was there. He had come early, parked his expensive automobile close to the start and finish lines, pulled off his suit coat and stood visiting with other local dignitaries.

The course was a beautiful one. It began and ended on a hilltop which overlooked a vast section of high desert. With binoculars you could see approximately three fourths of the course. The race began with the runners charging down off of that hilltop - a very sharp descent for at least two hundred yards - then breaking off into the plateau of rocks, cactus and desert scrub.

It was easy to see Tim, even when he was a long way off you could see the sun on that red hair and white body. He was leading but he had a dark shadow, never too far away. Every watcher forgot the other runners as they watched the magnificent dual between these opposites.

When they reached the bottom of the long, heartbreaking incline which led to the finish line, Tim was twenty or thirty feet ahead, a comfortable lead, but the Mexican American boy had apparently planned his race that way. With a supreme effort, he made up over half the distance which separated them before Tim became aware that he was making a move. Both boys were nearing exhaustion and Tim's attempt to increase his speed to hold off his challenger was feeble. Only five feet separated them as they came within fifty yards of the finish. Tim's father and the rest of the crowd had moved down the hill - everyone yelling encouragement to their champion.

The boys seemed to be moving in slow motion. They felt, I'm sure, that they were really moving, but I could have easily out run either of them that last fifty yards. They had already given their best in out distancing all other competitors. It is a marvelous thing to be able to stand that close - to be within touching distance, to actually feel the effort, the emotion, to be able to see every drop of sweat, every muscle movement, every line of the face, to feel the rhythm, the grim determination -

it was magnificent.

Tim was going to lose, I could sense it. The Mexican American boy had more energy left and his short, quick stride was more suited to the uphill grade than Tim's. I think Tim sensed it too, and the agony on his face was heart breaking. He was doing his best, he had nothing left to give. His dad was running beside him, red faced with anger, heedless of the spectacle he made, he screamed, *Don't you let that* _____ *beat you!* The last fifty yards seemed to last forever, but it ended. The Mexican American boy passed Tim five yards from the finish line and won by two feet.

Tim crossed the finish line and both boys sagged in absolute exhaustion, surrounded by coaches, officials, family and well wishers, with one exception. Tim's father had gone directly to his car and left in disgust. There was no embrace, no *I'm proud of you,* or *you'll get him next time,* no encouragement, laughter, or coming together. Tim's dad missed a great moment, a great opportunity- one that is seldom repeated.

A few minutes later, Lincoln came in. I ran up the hill beside him. He was as totally exhausted as any of the winners. He had given his best. Possibly two or three minutes separated him from the winners - a very small space in the length of a life time.

We left together- pleased with each other.

The Winner

I WAS WATCHING SOME LITTLE kids play soccer. I don't have little ones anymore so I just watch them - and their parents. These kids were about five or six. They were playing a real game - a serious game - two teams of them, complete with coaches, uniforms and parents. I didn't know any of them so I could enjoy the game without the distraction of being anxious about winning or losing -

I wish the parents and coaches could.

The teams were pretty evenly matched. I will just call them team one and team two. The first period passed with nobody scoring. The kids were hilarious. They were clumsy and terribly inefficient. They fell over their own feet, they would kick at the ball and miss it, they stumbled over it - but they didn't seem to care.

It was fun.

In the second quarter, the team one coach pulled out what must have been his first team and put in the scrubs, except for his best player who now guarded the goal. The game took a dramatic turn. I guess winning is important - even when you're five years old, because the team two coach left his best players in and the team one scrubs were no match for them. They swarmed around the little guy who was now the team one goalie. He was an outstanding athlete, but he was no match for three or four boys who were also very good. They began to score. He gave it everything he had, throwing his body recklessly trying to stop them. They scored two goals in quick succession. It infuriated him, he became a raging maniac, shouting, running, diving - but just as he would cover one boy with the ball, that boy would kick it to another boy twenty feet away and by the time he got there it was too late - they scored a third goal.

I soon learned who his parents were. They were nice, decent looking people. I could tell that his dad had just come from the office - he still had his suit and tie on. They yelled encouragement to their son. I became totally absorbed, watching the boy on the field and his parents on the sidelines.

After the third goal the little kid changed. He could see it was no use, he couldn't stop them, and he became frustrated. He didn't quit, but he became quietly desperate -

futility was written all over him.

After the fourth goal, I knew what was going to happen. I have seen it before. **He needed help so badly** and **there was none.** He retrieved the ball from the net and handed it to the referee – and then he cried. He just stood there and huge tears rolled down both cheeks. He went to his knees – put his fists to his eyes – his grief and frustration were so great – and he cried the tears of the helpless and broken hearted.

After the third goal his father changed too. He had been urging his son to try harder – yelling advice and encouragement. But then he changed. He became anxious. He tried to say that it was okay, to hang in there, he was grieving for the pain in his son.

When the boy went to his knees I saw the father start onto the field. His wife clutched his arm and said, *Jim, don't. You'll embarrass him*. He tore loose from her and ran onto the field. He wasn't supposed to – the game was still in progress. Suit, tie, dress shoes and all, he charged onto the field and he picked up his son so everybody would know that it was his boy, and he hugged him and held him and cried with him. I've never been so proud of a man in my life.

He carried him off the field and when he got close to the sidelines I heard him say, *Scotty, I'm so proud of you. You were great out there, I wanted everybody to know that you were my son.*

Daddy, the boy sobbed, *I couldn't stop them – I tried, Daddy, I tried and tried and they scored on me.*

*Scotty, it doesn't matter how many times they scored on you. You're my son and I'm proud of you. I want you to go back and play right now, **you can't stay out of the game**, and you're going to get scored on again, it **doesn't matter to us.** Go on now.*

It made a difference – I could tell it did. **When you're all alone**, and you're getting scored on – and you can't stop them – **it means a lot** to know that it doesn't matter to those who love you. The little guy ran back on to the field – and they scored two more times–
but it was okay.

Here's the pay-off. I get scored on every day. I try so hard. I throw my body recklessly in every direction. I fume and rage. I struggle with temptation and sin with every ounce of my being – and Satan laughs – and he scores again and the tears come, and I go to my knees – sinful, convicted, helpless. And my Father – my Father rushes right out on the field – right in front of the whole crowd – the whole jeering, laughing world – and He picks me up and He hugs me and He says,

John, I'm so proud of you. You were great out there. I wanted everybody here to know that you were My son,

and because I control the outcome of
this game, I declare you –

The Winner

The Price of Victory

IT WAS FRIDAY NIGHT and it was late. The field house was empty, except for us of course. We came because it was our last chance. One last game – just for old time's sake. We were moving. At least I was. We had played basketball so often here, that we had memorized the scratches in the glass backboard and the grooves in the parquet floors. Summer, winter, seasons did not matter to us,
                    it was year-round basketball.
    I had been playing with the boys since they were big enough to throw the ball high enough to score. Sometimes we just practiced – sometimes I played both of them – sometimes we played with others – most of the time, we played one on one. I always let them shoot, encouraged them and coaxed them. I could have blocked their shots easily. I let them score, gave them every possible advantage – at first, it was no contest, and it was fun,
                    we didn't even keep score.
    When the oldest boy was in junior high, it began to get a little competitive. Between the two of them, they could push me if I relaxed too much. The older boy would get angry with the younger one when he messed up – it wasn't quite as much fun, but still fun,
                    even though we now kept score.
    The years passed, all too quickly, the older boy was a high school senior and the younger a freshman. Now, it was an all-out war. I really had to work to beat both of them – elbowing, shoving – using superior height, weight and experience, and even then sometimes they won. There was much arguing over lane violations, offensive fouls, who touched the ball last before it went out of bounds, and nobody encouraged anybody. The loser sulked all the way home and it wasn't fun anymore.

Only the score was important.

The oldest boy went away to college. I was relieved. I only had to play one of them, and he was much less aggressive than his brother. The games were slower, we didn't push and foul each other so much and it was fun again - for a while. Then, he began to grow. When he was a junior he was as tall as I - but still not too aggressive. When he was a senior, he was taller and becoming very strong. He could out-jump me, his shooting touch was much improved, and his determination showed marked changes. The games were very close, and the arguing came back. The fun disappeared - except for winning -

and that can be very unrewarding.

He went to college where his older brother went, but we moved there. For three years we played together, separately, with others, but mostly -

one on one.

Tonight was the first time that it was really obvious. I was working my head off, sweat running from every pore, legs trembling from hustling loose balls - giving it everything I had. He was cruising, he was letting me shoot, giving me rebounds, keeping me in the game, trying to keep the score close -

he was carrying me!

Once again - it was no contest, the cycle was complete, and the fun came back,

I was enjoying myself.

God forgive me for taking the fun out of it, for purchasing my victories at the expense of their losses and achieving my satisfaction at the price of their agony. Help them to realize early

what I have learned too late, that -
the pleasure must be
in the playing -
in being together -
that winning and losing
often destroy the best
that life has to offer.

I wouldn't want to do it again –
raise my kids I mean,

but doing it has created a wonder –

a sense of dependance on God,

an appreciation for prayer
and providence

an understanding of love that I
would never have known

without it.